Special reissue offer of:

SET FREE
The Book About Hair
by Richard Stein (with Stephaine Cook)

and

Split|Ends
A Woman's Life With Her Hair
by Richard Stein

From Richard Stein, internationally renowned authority on beauty and innovator of the natural, balanced look in hair, comes the most stunning hair-care book ever—a gorgeous, state-of-the-art compendium of hair-care tips and techniques that will set you free to look great...because looking great is the best revenge.

Whether they're presidents of corporations, stars of the stage and screen, or ordinary people, Richard Stein's clients all look great—even when they're on the run, with no time to spare for their hair. Their secret? Stein's unique, natural, *no-fuss* techniques for beautiful hair.

Now, for the first time, Stein lets you in on his professional secrets. Beautifully illustrated with sumptuous photographs and line drawings, *Set Free* shows you the natural, balanced way to keep your hair looking terrific—without making constant trips to your hair stylist or spending hours in front of the mirror. You'll learn:

- The no bother—just beauty—way to clean, condition, and dry your hair
- The way to select a cut that expresses your own unique individuality, accents your hair's natural body—and can be restyled easily for all occasions
- Dozens of easy-to-prepare home recipes for hair-care products that are all-natural—and better than anything you can buy
- And much more

Your hair projects your personality to the world, and it's a vital component of your success and self-esteem. With Richard Stein's unique "wash and wear" strategies for beautiful hair, you can have it all: the knowledge and confidence that come with looking great—and an active, rewarding life that's free of complicated hair routines.

(continued from front flap)

British-born Richard Stein brings years of European expertise to the art of cutting and caring for hair. One of the pioneers of wash-and-wear hair since the sixties, Stein is committed to an individualized, natural look in hair that excludes rollers, hairspray, and all the other paraphernalia of the old-style beauty culture.

Drawing on an early interest in botanicals, Stein personally devised his own hair-care line, *Fleuremedy,* which he compounds from flowers and herbs for his exclusive clientele.

A multifaceted artist, Stein engages in a variety of creative pursuits, including writing music and lyrics, sculpting, and acting. All of these endeavors, he believes, feed into his main work: setting people free from their hair problems.

Richard Stein's salon is located at 1018 Lexington Avenue in New York City.

Stephen Grillo

Jacket design by Joel Avirom

Printed in U.S.A. Copyright © 1988 Simon & Schuster Inc.

SET FREE
The Book About Hair

by **Richard Stein**
with Stephanie Cook
Published by Simon and Schuster, 1988

Photography by Stephen Grillo
Illustrations by Donald Cann

CREDITS

Ellen Fink of Ariane, Boston
Inez and Colleen of Serenella, Boston
Kate Hines, designer of Kate Hines Jewelry
Mrs. Bernadette Pollick for her collection of antique lingerie

Copyright 1988 by Richard Stein and Lethal Gifts, Inc.
All rights reserved, including the right of reproduction in whole or in part in any form.

DESIGNED BY JOEL AVIROM

All herbal ingredients in this book can be found in health food stores or health food departments in supermarkets.

INTRODUCTION

Freedom is a concept that is fundamental to our lives ... and freedom is the idea behind this book, freedom to be yourself--truly and fully yourself--and still look as good as you can look. Freedom from the traditional female "enslavement" to those instruments of beauty torture--curlers, teasing, hairspray, blow-dryers--and from weekly visits to some dictatorial hairdresser obsessed with what this season's self-styled opinion makers have decreed "fashionable."

Setting people free from their problems with their hair is the single most challenging, and most rewarding, part of my daily work. Because, after all, looking great is the best revenge.

The title of this book was inevitable. It is a phrase I hear every day: "My God, Richard. You've set me *free!*" It is a phrase *I listen* for every day. Because a woman who gets up out of my chair for the first time must feel, somehow, that from this moment on her relationship with her hair is changed forever. She should be able to see herself in an entirely new way: as someone as much in charge of her hair--her looks--as she is in charge of the other crucially important aspects of her life.

Grandiose? I don't think so. Psychologists tell us that a woman's way of dealing with her hair--and especially the choice of style--is the single most revealing physical indicator of her feeling about herself, reflecting her attitudes toward her femininity, her status, her autonomy. In my long experience, I have never had any reason to think that this is not so. And I myself--after spending my life in this business--would go even further ... because I would say that attitudes toward one's hair and the choices one makes about hairstyling not only reflect these things, but *often determine* them.

The idea of being able to transform someone with just the right haircut is what gives me creative impetus. When people are secure about their hair and how it looks, it can free up many other aspects of their lives: their "style," their self-image, even their sense of self-worth. And once these things are affected, there is often a spectacular ripple effect on other things--career, relationships, even a sense of personal mastery.

This may be why so many of my clients come from worlds driven by power, charisma, and competence: heads of corporations and almost heads; politicians; psychoanalysts and therapists; and people in every branch of the arts--artist and gallery owners; writers, agents, and editors; producers, directors, and "stars of stage and screen." They--as well as all the regular folk caught up in these exhilarating times--are all terribly busy, no-nonsense people who live on tight time budgets and want hair that is easily and instantly put to rights, is a snap to take care of, and always looks entirely wonderful.

What I do, very simply, is sculpt hair. I try to make cutting it into an art form--understanding the material I am working with (different in each case), knowing what aspect of the person I am trying to express, and doing both these things with sensitivity and skill. The women and men who come to my salon leave with their own very personal "hair sculpture" that transcends the latest fashion dictates and becomes the basis for the creation of a unique sense of style.

Style itself never goes *out* of style (although fashion, by definition, does), so my clients always look up-to-date. From my perspective, this means that my work remains fresh in execution and challenging and interesting on a day-to-day level.

For a client, part of this exercise is learning to love her or his hair *just as it is*. I am often amazed at how few people really know what their own hair is like: what type it is, what can be done with it, how easily it can be taken care of.

I was one of the pioneers of the "natural" look--the blow-and-go, wash-and-wear trend in hairstyling--and when I first let my own hair go naturally full and curly way back in the geometric sixties (when it was the "straights" and nothing but the "straights") people used to stop me in elevators and accost me at parties and ask to touch my hair... which made me wary of being in close quarters, but eventually less uptight about having my hair touched.

Hairwise, this is a more tactile, easygoing time for women than ever before in history. The days of the week-long, tormented-and-sprayed "solid" hairset are gone (thank heavens!). Women today lead high-stress lives that don't include a clockwork visit to the beauty parlor to get "redone"; that time now goes to the exercise class or graduate seminar or therapist. Women today have a far better understanding of what they want from their lives, and more and more of them are willing to forgo those old "constructed" looks for something more natural, more comfortable. *Freer*.

The information in this book is designed to liberate you from all the nonsense about hair and to bring a sense of confidence and self-esteem to your relationship with your own hair. It should be wearer-friendly. It doesn't need to be tamed; it needs to be discovered and then celebrated.

Because I care as much about what is *in* your head as what is *on* it.

Looking Great is the Best Revenge

PART 1

THE STEIN WAY

This book is different from anything else you may have read about taking care of your hair, cutting it, or figuring out the "right style" for you.

This book is about seeing yourself in a new way as a "wearer" of your hair, and it's about my particular methods for making that hair healthier and more beautiful. It also includes recipes for dozens of my natural "remedies." This book is meant to be a guide and a resource. And in the final assessment, it is about a lot more than just hair.

With the right cut and correct information, you should be able to sleep on your hair, run your hands through it, wash it and dry it in no time. It will feel better on your head, you will spend less time and money attending to it, and you will feel more in control.

After all, that's the whole point, isn't it? To be self-reliant?

There are two "philosophical principles" that could be said to reflect my signature way of working with hair; both are central to the decision-making process in my creative partnership with a client:

1. a commitment to NATURALNESS
2. a great respect for the concept of BALANCE.

These principles do not separate out neatly; they overlap and are interdependent, as you will see when I talk about them. In fact, they are complementary--in a sense a single perspective on how your hair should feel on your head, how it should be handled, and what it should do in the creation and maintenance of a particular way of seeing *yourself*.

But let me explain more about the Stein way.

Naturalness and balance. You can see why-how--they're related. Hair should both be a vehicle for self-expression and "reveal" its own character. Hair that is hard to handle, or must be fixed constantly or endlessly fussed with, is not doing its job--that is, *expressing* you and making you more comfortable with yourself. Nothing should interfere with your pleasure in wearing your hair, and if it is "taken care of"--if you feel balanced, pulled together, at ease--there is one less thing to worry about and one more thing that encourages you to get on with the important business in your life.

NATURAL HAIR AND HAIR CARE

I've always been dedicated to the belief that natural hair care would enhance natural beauty and keep hair alive longer. My purpose in my work has been to get "nature" back into hair: natural treatment products you can make yourself, natural methods of care and enhancement, natural "styling," and a natural look.

It's important to emphasize right away that the idea of natural treatment products you can make at home-where you can control quality and freshness--is very close in concept to the idea of a natural look. In both cases I am talking about appreciating and making use of something in its most basic, most self-expressive, most "real" state, whether that something is the conditioner you blend fresh from flower petals and honey, or the hair you are going to learn to accept for what it is. This is how I came to develop my own shelf-stable products-the Fleuremedy line.

When I first had my own salon and was in a position to do--and use--things I really believed in, I began to explore the potential of hair care products that were as close to natural as possible. Initially, I spent a good deal of time raiding the health food stores. Their products were--for the most part--acceptable, but it made intuitive sense to me that whatever I could make *fresh* would be even better: after all, if you make something yourself, you have absolute control over what goes into it. And you have absolute control over its freshness.

Perhaps because I was raised in England, I grew up with a profound love for gardening and the cultivation of flowers and herbs. This is probably how I first became interested in applying my knowledge of herbs and flowers to hair care.

But you will see how this works later, in the sections of this book that teach you how to take care of your hair....

I see hair simply as another substance to be worked with--and understood--much the way fabric, or stone, or even raked gravel of a Zen garden is worked with. Trying to understand hair this way, I work with it much as I would arrange flowers. The right balance can free my client and make her aware of all the positive and unique qualities her hair possesses.

BALANCE--MAKING THINGS EASY

A good haircut-the *right* haircut for you-will not only be balanced in the way it looks and feels on your head, it will "balance" your whole presentation of yourself. It has to do with the experience you will have of your own hair when it is cut in such a way that every single hair is balanced on your head. The sensation of the head is changed, and you will feel *yourself* balanced.

Take a cowlick, for example--or what some people think of as a "lump" of hair that never seems to do what you want it to. It can be anywhere on your head, but you are always somehow conscious of it. You may feel that all your life you have had to "deal with" that lump of hair, and it is forever in the back of your mind as an aspect of yourself that somehow "unbalances" you ... and by implication, keeps you from being fully and comfortably yourself. When you are finally "balanced" with just the right cut, it can be a revelation. Something that kept you off balance (literally) has been set right, has been attended to. Balance is beautiful. It's as simple as that.

HIDING IN YOUR HAIR

*T*he phrase most often heard by a hairdresser (not counting "Oh, just do what you want"--which can be a bald-faced lie as well as a veiled challenge) is "Not too short!" or "I only want an *inch* off." Although every style can benefit from a trim every six weeks or so, the sad fact is that most women get their hair cut too infrequently ... and let it go too long between cuts. Hanging on to all that hair is often a symptom of hiding-- usually from yourself.

Getting in touch. Being honest. Sometimes it's hard to do things the easy way. That's where I come in. Because my job is much more than just cutting hair. I try to see the whole person, to help her see herself. I take a very active role in the process of beauty transformation.

The kind of woman who tends to say, "I'm not a good-looking person; I don't have this or that," gets so locked into her insecurities that she can't experiment.

GETTING STUCK

*W*omen often "freeze" their look to reflect a particular time in their lives when they knew they looked great--or *thought* they looked great--

and begin to build their self-image around that one secure moment. There is real danger in this.

You can see when this happens to certain movie stars who stop allowing their looks to evolve naturally and begin to look like older and older versions of their younger selves. *Sometimes* this qualifies as real style--as understanding who you are and what you want to say about yourself like Katharine Hepburn, Lauren Bacall, or Claudette Colbert. More frequently, it comes from "freezing up," from a fear that they are losing what was precious to them about themselves (youth ... beauty). So they freeze. And you can see them years later--decades later--looking like cartoon caricatures of the women they once were.

The most satisfying challenge I can meet is to bring a woman into the present with just the right cut.

LEARNING TO UNDERSTAND THE CLIENT

*F*undamental to a good cut (and any other major styling decision) is the understanding of a client's vulnerabilities and insecurities--that vital need to be reassured. Thus a great deal of sensitivity is required, not only so the "right" decisions about what is to be done with someone's hair will get made, but so that each person I deal with is handled with the utmost gentleness, courtesy, and insight.

So what is about to take place is almost magical: a new hairstyle (like a different makeup, or a face-lift, or a weight loss) hints at an adventure into unexplored dimensions of the image you hold of yourself. There is always the hope, of course, that this "change" will go far beyond a "new look," and that the new look in turn will open up your self-perceptions ...

that you will see yourself as you never have before, and that other people will respond to the transformation in a way that will make you more secure, or more accepted, or more loved.

And I am expected to be the agent of this transformation. As my grandma would say, Oy, vey!

TAKING THE STEP TOGETHER: TWO CASE HISTORIES

A step like this--a commitment to change, and even adventure--can be exhilarating or it can be disastrous. And which one of the two it is depends a great deal on the quality of our "partnership"; it depends on my insight and on your willingness to let yourself be "seen" and then worked with.

I think of one new client in particular.

My immediate impression (the incomplete analysis) on first meeting this woman was that she was overweight and had a curtain of long hair that fell forward over one eye. She was, in fact, a woman in hiding.

But what I saw when I concentrated on her face was ... Garbo. This wasn't idle flattery; it was the structure on which I began to construct my working impressions.

This process of intuiting some likeness can give hope to a woman, so it's a hunch I use fairly often. It also gives a sense of security to someone who is new to working with me. She feels "discovered" because she knows I can "see" her as she might be at her best. You help someone like this make a change when you lend her confidence--right up front--that you care and are making an effort. Why? Because someone who doesn't feel you care is going to have a hard time trusting you. I need to *participate* in whatever she is feeling--her insecurity, her fear, her hope. I look at the face, I look at the clothes, I read the body language, each tells me a great deal about what kind of person this is--how she feels about herself, how far I can go with my vision. I look everywhere I can for clues and allow myself to feel for some kind of resolution.

This particular woman, for instance, had expensive clothes, beautiful jewelry, an imposing carriage, a lovely face. Her hair was an exquisite natural color, a sort of taupe, but it was so long and shapeless it dragged down everything about her, making her look worn out and virtually obscuring her face. (It turned out she had been cutting it herself--and very little at that, from the look of it--for many years. In all, it was in terrible condition.) She also came dressed entirely in black--a black designer tent-that she presumably thought hid her body. There was a stunning woman there, buried under layers of silk and flesh and hair.

This "uncovering" was a radical change for her ... and a great risk to take. When she saw the first hank of hair go, she told me she was going to faint. I didn't fall for this,. I simply told her in that case she'd better lie down on the salon floor. But what happened in the course of a drastic cut was a revelation. Ten years were lopped off along with the foot of hair, and her new chin-length look took advantage not only of the loveliness of her face, but of her really beautiful hair. Suddenly the person in the mirror was gone, replaced by an embryonic new image, the insecurity by a glimmer of hope.

Now, *every time* this woman passes a mirror, her reflection reassures her that she is indeed beautiful. There is that constant reinforcement for both herself *and me*.

This story has a happy ending. The entire transformation, which took some eighteen months, finally included new makeup to complement the hair (it was, after all, the first time in years her face was really *seen*), an astonishing loss of weight, and a new wardrobe that said "I am a beautiful woman, and I know it." It was wonderful to participate in this incredible metamorphosis.

There is another type of woman who brings me a very different kind of "partnership" potential: she looks the way she thinks she looks already. Let me explain.

This woman has been to one too many hairdressers. She knows what it is about, is ready to "take me on." What she is looking for is reinforcement and acknowledgment that what she has been doing is right, that she is terrific looking. What she is *not* looking for is a challenge: she will probably insist on giving me instructions all the way through the haircut, because *she knows what she wants*.

The challenge with someone like this is to help her see *more*, to learn more, to go beyond where she is. In the larger sense, it is critical to appreciate-as I said-that there is *always* more. This is what growth is all about.

That inner image--the one that propels you when you get up in the morning and do your makeup and your hair and get dressed, the one that drives you--is very precious. And what I do for the experienced woman-the one with the strong intact image, the fully realized, consonant sense of self-is to fulfill that image for her, to make it manifest...and then to push beyond it. She is allowing me to explore her fantasies on her behalf, then bring reality into line with the fantasy.

It is still the same creative partnership. We just start farther down the road in the matter of transformation.

EXPRESSING YOURSELF WITH YOUR HAIR

Building a new self-image--or improving on an old one--is a big challenge and an intimidating step to take, no matter how secure you feel. I have spent enough time with enough people to understand that just because you are powerful, or important, or famous, or wealthy, doesn't mean that when it comes to your appearance you aren't frightened and insecure, overly sensitive, and in need of help and special handling.

A personal style change is especially intimidating when it involves hair: makeup can be wiped off or thrown out; a fashion mistake can be returned, shoved to the back of a closet, or given away. But once you have submitted to the ministrations and vision of a hairdresser, you may find yourself stuck with an error of minor or major proportions. Your hair, after all, must be worn all the time.

In fact, it is my opinion that hair has become the crucial element in the creation of a strong sense of personal style.

ESTABLISHING A RELATIONSHIP

Getting your hair attended to is much like the consumption of any service, from car repair to medical attention--the more you involve yourself in the decisions being made, and the better informed you are about what goes into the decision, the better the service you will ultimately get.

First you need to find the right person--a person you can trust with your hair. Then you need to know how to prepare yourself to make the hairdresser's job easier and yourself more comfortable--in short, how to make that partnership a success--by being aware of how to present yourself at the salon, which questions to ask and which directions to give (should any need giving), and what a good cut looks and feels like.

I often think that if you are prepared in these ways, and then trust your instincts and judgment, things can't help but go swimmingly. It is as important to know how to be a good client as it is to be a good stylist.

FINDING THE RIGHT PERSON

Unless you live in New York of Los Angeles, it is hard to do research by scanning the fashion or life-style magazines or picking up names from designers' shows. It is not impossible to find "your" hairdresser through these more formal channels, but neither is it particularly easy. Or necessarily efficient.

I think it is much better to trust hairstyling you see on a real live human being. Every day you probably see other people with healthy, shiny hair and a cut you admire. The best way I know of to do research is to start asking *every one* of these people where they go to have their hair done, and who at the salon actually did it. (You will probably find that a couple of the same names keep turning up.) When you feel you have collected enough names--or have heard the same one often enough--drop by the salon(s) and see how you feel about the ambience and the atmosphere of communication you sense between the people working there and the patrons.

You can find out a great deal this way, so don't skimp on this stage of your research.

CONSULT FIRST

Once you've settled on a hairdresser, you will probably feel anxious to get in and get on with it. To avoid any sort of disappointment, however, the absolutely best thing to do--in my opinion--is to arrange for a consultation prior to an actual cut ... or perm ... or change of color.

There is an advantage to arranging for a separate interview *before* you even make that appointment to have something done to your hair: neither you nor the hairdresser is under any pressure to make an on-the-spot decision about what to do with your hair. You can have a more leisurely discussion about your own needs and goals and really focus on what you would like to have done rather than rush to get on with it; plus you can begin to establish a sense of whether you and a particular stylist are compatible or not.

A prior consultation also gives you the opportunity to show pictures if you have brought them-of a former hairstyle you particularly liked on yourself and would like to work toward if you are growing your hair, for instance, or some examples of hairstyles you like on others. I love seeing any pictures a client has chosen. They are very revealing and can help me understand what she has in mind. It doesn't mean you will end up looking like a specific picture, or that we will even decide to use the picture as a point of reference. It does help me to see what sort of thing appeals to you and gives us a common basis on which to discuss what it is you are looking for in your hair.

Some women, of course, have little sense of the "appropriateness" of particular hairstyles for them--the forty-year-old woman, for instance, who has decided she wants to look like the latest rock-star sensation. As the hairdresser, I have to decide quickly why she sees this look as being right for her or what aspects of it she is particularly drawn to and then decide whether there are ways in which it can be translated or adapted to her.

Sometimes I must say, "Sorry, in my opinion, nothing I see here is going to work for you." But then I can also say, "Tell me what about this you particularly like," so I get some sense of how this woman feels about herself and how I can give her something that will express her.

All in all, it's much easier to be speculative and creative if a drastic change is not imminent, if you are in a position to say that you want to go home and think over a suggestion. It takes the pressure off both stylist and client.

Having a consultation before making an appointment for the actual cut has other advantages. If you do come back, you are going to feel ever-so-slightly more comfortable because it will be the second instead of the first time you and the hairdresser will have met and worked together. You'll have had the opportunity to mull over any suggestions that may have been made. And both of you are surer of yourselves, so the communication during the cut should also go more smoothly, with fewer opportunities for misunderstanding.

If you don't feel comfortable with someone during the consultation, *don't go back*; this hairdresser isn't right for you, no matter how good (or "chic," or "in") s/he is supposed to be. You must be able to *communicate* with her or him just as you have to with any other person in your life whom you have hired to work for you.

THE QUALITY OF COMMUNICATION

*T*his testing of communication is your best guarantee of satisfaction. How are you treated? Does s/he seem interested in you and what your life is like? Are you listened to? *The quality* of the dialogue is critical.

The basic elements of the relationship should work themselves out in the first five or ten minutes of conversation. If you had communication problems with your previous hairdresser, don't be afraid to say so. Doing this establishes that you are not a sheep to be shorn, and that you have a basic right to ask questions about what the stylist intends to do ... and have them answered.

If you have booked an appointment to have something done, and for some reason--once you get there--you don't feel right, for heaven's sake, don't stay then, either. You should never feel pushed: it's your money, your time, your hair. Guilt should not be involved. If you feel guilty for canceling an appointment on the spot, pay the person: sometimes it's cheaper to give someone fifty dollars and not get butchered.

And trust your instincts! Too many women don't, and that's too bad, because women have great instincts and are probably safer following them than not. I believe very much in personal chemistry; if you sense something negative between you, or feel put down or insulted, you must trust those instincts, or you will in all likelihood be doubly sorry: you won't like what's done, and you'll feel like a fool because you knew it all the time.

THE GROWTH OF THE RELATIONSHIP

I find that as I get to know a woman, our sense of understanding and commitment to each other grows...and that is as it should be. It is, after all, a very charged situation; touching someone's head amounts to a sort of "psychic massage." Women especially are extraordinarily responsive to all this touching, and I am convinced it "opens" someone up, emotionally and psychologically--emotionally in that it inclines them to want to "make friends," to feel close to their hairdresser, and psychologically in that they begin to see new possibilities for themselves and are more receptive to their own potential. I truly believe there is something about having your head touched that "releases" you; it may sound strange, but I think it is nearly impossible for a woman not to be open with me when she is in my chair.

A note of caution, however: too many women go to a first session with someone new hoping to establish this rapport immediately. Now, while you should certainly be able to make judgments about a hairdresser's personal receptivity to you within the first few minutes, you cannot expect the kind of warmth and acceptance you will surely have after getting to know him or her. What you can reasonably expect is to be greeted cordially, made comfortable, and asked for your thoughts about your hair and some questions about your life-style (see the question agenda that follows). What you cannot expect is love at first sight.

It may sound wearyingly self-evident to say this, but simple politeness and respect for the hairdresser's experience go a long way toward laying the groundwork for a good, working, mutually supportive relationship.

And don't arrive in a sweatsuit, with your hair unwashed or uncombed. This doesn't help the hairdresser to see anything about you except that you're a mess. (I have insight, but even my imagination has some limits!) Do your hair yourself as best you can. Wear daytime makeup. A new hairdresser is going to take his or her measure of you by what s/he sees at this first meeting and make judgments that may affect how your hair ends up looking.

In short, the hairdresser's immediate impression of you should be how you see yourself *at your best*.

THE HAIR AGENDA

*P*art of my job is to make information available to people. Information about hair, about style, about solving or caring for special problems. About *their* hair and style and problems.

These are the most "basic" questions about hair. Are you growing it in? Are you cutting it off? Are you tired of coloring (either the process or the product of the process)? Have you permed, and do you want to continue?

Here are some of the questions I run through with a new client ... and periodically with people I have been cutting for a time:

1

How do you see yourself? What is your life like at home, on the job, at play.

- How do you feel about your hair?
- Are there any particular hairstyles you are interested in at this time? Have you brought pictures?
- When have you last really liked your hair? What was its style then? Did you bring pictures?

2

Changes in your hair:

- Do you want to continue to color, perm ... ?
- Would you like to grow your hair longer? Conversely, are you specifically looking for something shorter?
- Would you like to give me carte blanche? Are you ready for a brand-new look?

3

Why are you switching hairdressers? How would you like me to be different from your previous one?

4

How much do you really know about your hair?

- Do you know what type of hair you have? (You would be surprised how many people have no idea.... I'll talk about this later.)
- What do you feel are your hair's "weakest" points? (cowlicks? thinning? a damaged patch?)
- Do you know what color your hair *really* is? (And are you willing to go two months without coloring to find out?)
- Are you aware of exactly what your hair does if you just wash it, comb it through, and leave it to dry naturally? (It beats me why so many people are afraid even to try this!)

It's not *just* that I'm nosy; your life-style *is* a critical factor to our successful collaboration.

HANDLING MISUNDERSTANDINGS

*T*here may be some disagreements. That's life. You should not, however, ever have to tolerate a tantrum from a hairdresser. Although many of us are by nature temperamental, you are the paying customer, and it is you who should have the final say.

I have heard so many stories about the first cut that is going well--the weather has been discussed, a few anecdotes have been told, some personal history has been exchanged--when you do something as presumptuous as commenting on the course of the cut or perhaps requesting that it not be too short.... Suddenly the communicative Dr. Jekyll becomes a raving Mr. Hyde, hurling his brush at the mirror and screaming at you. My advice in this situation is simply to get up out of the chair (even if you are half-cut or your hair is wet) and explain calmly that you cannot tolerate such behavior, nor can you trust someone so excitable to finish the cut. Dress, and leave without paying the bill.

Of course it takes guts to do this; but the confrontation rarely gets this far. Usually the hairdresser will realize s/he has lost control with the wrong person and will apologize and calm down. It is a hard stand to take--and not a comfortable one for most women, who are much more used to acquiescing because they don't want to cause a scene--but it will do you good. You will also help the hairdresser to put things back in perspective.

While this kind of thing doesn't happen often, if and when it does, you should have your response prepared just in case. Don't allow yourself to be pushed around. The salon is as good a place as any to begin assertiveness training.

YOUR NEW LOOK

Question: So what happens when you finally get the great cut that is going to change your life? Answer: Look over that whole "mix" of your self-presentation with a cold eye. A good place to start is by asking the person who has cut your hair for his or her advice about wardrobe and (especially!) makeup.

Cutting bangs begs for more "eye"; hair newly revealing the temple may require lipstick if you have worn none. And if you change your hair color, you almost certainly will need to adjust the shades of your makeup palette. One way or another, makeup frequently does have to be redone. We do it at the salon and, increasingly, so do many other hairdressers. It is an appropriate part of a full-service business where self-image is concerned.

Advice might not be offered without your asking. So don't be shy--ask. Maybe you'll find out something that will make you look better, make your hair look better, and allow you to have the total good feeling about yourself that you deserve.

PART 2
HEALTHY HAIR– The Natural Way

CHAPTER 1

The Basics

THE HAIR'S STRUCTURE

Hair is protein, like fingernails. And even the liveliest head of hair is dead material, alive only at its source in the scalp. Any preparation you apply, therefore, can affect the hair itself only to the extent that it cleans, conditions, smooths, or protects the hair shaft and its cuticles. And while this can improve hair's appearance enormously, any real nourishment

comes from the hair follicle, the scalp, and the blood supply to both, which feeds the emerging hair shaft (although what you put on your hair may affect both the *look* of the surface of the hair and the condition of the scalp). This is why nutrition and massage are each an important part of my philosophy.

A strand of hair is made up of a number of layers, wound like insulation around a core. The layers--and their shape (a round cross section is typical of straight hair, and a flattened one of curly hair)--determine hair texture (fine to coarse) and color (bleaching, for instance, removes the colored layers of darker hair). The *number* of hairs determines what is thought of as "thickness." Thick and thin, fine and coarse, are concepts that are frequently confused.

It is the outermost layer of the hair shaft that most determines how your hair actually *looks* how shiny and healthy it seems. This is the *cuticle*, the keratinized layer of the hair. The cuticle is really a series of overlapping scales. When these scales are not disrupted by damage to the hair, they lie flat and are smooth and shiny. When they have been abused by heat, chemicals, or rough treatment, however, they begin to look (under a microscope) like a shingled roof that has been through a bad storm--chipped, bent, awry, or broken off altogether. This is what causes frizz, dullness, split ends, and the "fried" look of some people's hair.

Cleaning or conditioning substances that smooth these "scales" down--fill the gaps with protein, silicon, or waxes and coat the hair strand to prevent further damage--help hair to look shiny, be manageable, and feel soft. But the healthiest-looking hair is going to have to be *healthy when it emerges from the scalp*; what you eat, how long and how well you sleep and exercise, and the quality of the blood supply to the forming hair will determine the health, strength, and beauty of each and every strand.

THE ROLE OF NUTRITION

A great deal has been written about how the chemical composition of the hair reflects general health...just as the condition of your skin and nails says a great deal about the shape you're in and how you've been feeling. This is *fundamentally* true. There is as yet, however, no definitive proof that what you eat, or the environment in which you live, will be *accurately* reflected in the chemical makeup of the hair (in spite of what hair analysts would like you to believe).

While it is only reasonable to be wary of extravagant claims for treating hair by regulating intake of certain vitamins and minerals, I do think it highly sensible to assume that what you eat will make a difference in how your hair looks. For heaven's sake--we all know it makes a difference in how you feel!

My nutritional advice sounded a lot more radical a decade ago than it does now; then, limiting one's red meat intake and concentrating on grains and fresh vegetables and fruit was still a hallmark of the wild-eyed, Earth-Shoe-wearing fringe. Now it is generally accepted. So much the better. Your hair will be much improved--as will your skin and body functioning generally--by shifting toward this lighter, more natural way of eating.

Supplemental vitamins I especially recommend for the maintenance of the good looks and health of your hair are A and E (in fact, E is of considerable help applied *externally* to trouble spots on scalp; more on this later). I recommend 400 units a day of E, and a "minimum daily requirement" (MDR) supplement of A. (You have to be careful not to take too much A, which can be toxic at high levels.) Other vitamins that affect the health of your hair are B complex (a good standard "stress B" should do it) and C (about 750 mg. every three hours--C is water soluble, and any excess is quickly discarded by the body--is ideal, but who remembers? A time-release C is a good alternative).

Trace minerals for the hair that you might want to consider adding to any daily supplemental regime (especially after illness or other physical or emotional trauma) include zinc and iron. There is some thought that we lose trace minerals in our body as we age, and that some graying and hair loss can be caused by deficiencies of these two trace minerals. Start with the MDR dose.

Potassium and iodine levels must also be maintained for optimal hair health. PABA (para-aminobenzoic acid) the same chemical that is used as a sunscreen--also comes in tablets and, taken regularly in small doses, is said to be a substantial help in keeping hair from graying.

HAIR GROWTH AND HAIR FALL

*H*ow well and how fast hair grows depends on your genes, your age and your general state of health. Being an optimist, I tend toward the assumption that state of health (which you can do something about) is more important than genes...with the exception of male-pattern baldness, which is (sorry!) inherited. (A man should check out his mother's brother, who's a pretty accurate indication of what is in store, because baldness genes are supposedly carried on the female chromosome.)

The best thing I know to keep hair growing fast and strong is to make sure the scalp and all those infant hairs nestled in their follicles get a steady stream of oxygen and nutrients (nutrients you will have ensured by eating right and taking the appropriate supplements) from a good blood supply. Encourage this supply not only by exercising your body-- which picks up your metabolism in general and getting enough rest to counteract the modern plague of stress; you should also **step up local blood flow through scalp massage**. As far as I'm concerned, after eating well and keeping yourself in shape, the most critical impact on how your hair looks--as well as how fast it grows and how little of it you will lose--is directly attributable to the beneficial effects of massage. You can read all about it in Chapter 2.

Some hair loss, or hair fall, is a natural part of the renewal cycle of the scalp and hair--and can vary with season, menstrual cycle, and general health. You can expect a normal "shedding rate" of up to one hundred hairs a day; any more than this indicates a problem--almost always at the growth source in the scalp. It is also not unusual to experience hair loss one to three months after illness, childbirth, surgery, or a period of particular emotional stress and/or tension.

Hair loss and sometimes even skin infections may also be caused by physical trauma to the scalp--hair that is worn tightly pulled back, for instance, or too much teasing. Moreover, hair that is not trimmed regularly can get so dry at the ends that it tangles and so is pulled out with daily brushing and combing long before it is ready to give up the ghost (just one more good reason to have your hair trimmed every so often).

In cases where something does indeed seem to be wrong with your hair and there is no ready explanation like pregnancy or a recent illness, you might ask your hairdresser first whether s/he knows what might be causing the problem. If the problem remains unidentified, get to a trichologist (a hair specialist) if you live in a metropolitan area where these professionals are available, or to a dermatologist or your doctor. Sometimes hair loss is symptomatic of something more serious. I don't need to tell you that when you notice any substantial change in your physical self that is not readily explicable, you should immediately consult a medical professional.

HAIR TYPES

*H*air types are consistently misunderstood. As I mentioned earlier, the most basic misunderstanding is in the distinctions between fine and coarse, thick and thin. **Fine/coarse defines the diameter of a particular hair strand**, not straight or curly; either can be either--fine and straight (like most Nordic hair), fine and curly (like baby hair), coarse and straight (Oriental), or coarse and curly (black hair). Thick and thin is another blessing or problem--respectively. *Everyone wants thick* (although not coarse) hair; *everyone* worries about hair thinning with age, when the follicles begin to "tire out" and stop producing a luxuriant crop.

Thick hair may be hard to manage because of its weight. In cases where it is too heavy to sustain a style particularly when its growth pattern (all forward, for instance) is a problem or when it is extremely curly--it can be thinned judiciously to ease handling and encourage bounce and movement.

The real challenge to any hairdresser is not thick but *thin*--trying to make less look like more without resorting to hairpieces, wigs, or falls.

I will touch on creating the illusion of thick hair later, but just let me say one thing here that cannot be emphasized enough: **You don't make your hair look thicker by refusing to have it cut.** Just the opposite is true: hair that is trimmed regularly and attended to by someone who knows what s/he is doing will always look more luxuriant, healthier, and shinier than hair that is not.

CHAPTER 2

The Healthy Scalp

The scalp is the living support system of the hair. And a healthy scalp is the prerequisite to strong, shiny, healthy hair. Although your *hair* needs mainly to be stripped of dirt and oil and then protected--treated more like the finish on a fine piece of furniture--your scalp needs to be nourished

and stimulated, to be cleaned and toned and moisturized...just as your face does.

So your hair and scalp have significantly differing requirements for optimal care: what is good for the hair strand in terms of cleaning and protection (think of the detergent in shampoos, which may irritate the scalp--and the waxes in conditioners, which may coat it) is not necessarily what is going to be kindest to your scalp.

I have tried to get around this problem with my natural remedies. They are for scalp *and* hair--although not always in equal proportions--and unlike many preparations for the treatment of the hair alone, they *and their application* are especially beneficial to the scalp. And although I include a few of my special "scalp restoratives" here, you should be aware that--whatever else it may do--nearly **every recipe in this book nourishes the scalp**.

In some ways, the herbal preparations presented in this chapter and elsewhere are the most important feature of this book. They are certainly closest to my heart, as I have worked on the concept of natural remedies and developed the actual recipes from the time I started in this business. I am also fortunate enough to be able to bring what I know to people in the form of an actual line of products--the Fleuremedy line for hair--which is sold in my salon as well as carried by some of the more exclusive department stores in the country.

It was long a dream of mine to take what I knew and--literally--package it. I have done that, and now that the Fleuremedy line is available, my clients and other people who are interested in natural hair care have no excuse to pass up healthy, organic maintenance and treatment products when they don't want to fool around with herbs and a blender.

GENERAL DIRECTION FOR ALL RECIPES

Most of the dozens of recipes you'll find here and elsewhere are for single application amounts (exceptions are noted) natural ingredients without preservatives can quickly spoil or become rancid. By the same token, it is important that the recipe ingredients *themselves* be fresh; this means that once you have bought an oil, a vitamin, an herb, or some other dry ingredient, care must be taken in both handling and storage. The refrigerator (or freezer, for dry ingredients and some herbs) is usually the best place to keep natural, organic substances (even those--like bran--that don't "require" refrigeration), which should always be tightly covered and/or wrapped to keep it from drying out, becoming stale or picking up odors.

To repeat, *in general*, these preparations are not intended to be stored or saved. If you have very short hair, you may wish to halve the recipe.

ALLERGIC REACTIONS

Occasionally someone will have an allergic reaction to a preparation--natural or otherwise. If you know or suspect you are sensitive to an ingredient in a particular recipe, don't chance it. And while any food allergy you have may not manifest itself dermatologically, you should be aware of your body and its sensitivities. If you have reason to be concerned about a potential reaction, test a small patch of skin with a preparation before applying it to your hair and scalp. Your skin is just as capable of absorbing substances and chemicals as your digestive system is.

PREPARATION

You should, of course, use squeaky-clean utensils to mix your hair preparations. A small glass bowl or a Pyrex measuring cup is ideal. Avoid metal containers and tools; a metal may leach into the preparation in microscopic amounts or sometimes cause a subtle chemical reaction that can render the preparation less effective.

Use either a blender or a food processor to emulsify the preparation that requires it.

APPLICATION

These preparations are meant to be applied to--and then massaged into--clean hair and scalp. (See the following chapter on shampooing for the correct technique.) Your hair should not be wet but just barely damp (towel-dry, please...*and squeeze*, don't rub, the water out). Then give yourself a chance to relax while you let the recipe do its work: **apply, massage, and wrap hair in a towel**. Lie down briefly, if possible, with the feet higher than the head so that you relax and the blood goes to the head and scalp, hastening absorption of all the good ingredients in these natural remedies.

The massage techniques I describe later in this chapter are used in the application of the remedies. Massage is an important adjunct to these natural hair preparations. By stimulating the flow of blood to the scalp, it enhances the absorption of the nutrients in the preparation and at the same time refreshes and cleanses from the inside. Regular scalp massage will be of great benefit in giving you the kind of hair you want: glossy, full, lively.

Correct application is as important as the preparation itself. If you don't give your scalp the opportunity to absorb the nutrients you are providing it, and the hair shaft the benefit of the cleaning/glossing/protecting, you are only accomplishing half the job. Beyond that, giving yourself a few moments' respite from whatever else you are doing is just plain good for you. It's an ideal time to pamper the rest of yourself...including your mind. I personally find it particularly refreshing to meditate during a treatment.

RINSING OUT A PREPARATION

Almost as important as the integrity, freshness, and naturalness of the recipes themselves--and the massage for application, the relaxation during absorption--is the way in which you rinse out these cleaning, conditioning, and treatment preparations...or for that matter, rinse out *anything* you put on your hair and scalp. All the good things you "feed" your hair can be nullified by poor attention to removing substances that might dull the hair shaft and attract dust and dirt or stay on the scalp and cause irritation and/or shedding of the outer layer of epidermis. In some cases I have specified a "shampoo rinse" or special herbal rinse (see Chapter 3). In other cases you can rinse with pure tap water--if your water is soft and relatively free of chemicals and foreign matter--or bottled/distilled water if it is not.

Once you have prepared a special rinse water (which can be done in large batches--this will keep), you may want to have some of *that* in your refrigerator for use whenever you wish. You can also use a special rinse water after your regular rinsing in plain water to give your hair that extra-special boost and shine.

A WORD ABOUT THE INGREDIENTS

Most of these ingredients are available in your local health food store...and sometimes even in the large supermarkets that seem to pepper the exurban countryside. Some can be found in your own garden; others are more difficult to get and will require a resourceful pharmacist or your willingness to initiate a relationship with a vendor who deals in more unusual herbs, oils, and extracts. Those of us who live in New York City have Caswell-Massey and Kiehl's Pharmacy at our disposal; other cities may also have their herbalists, natural hygienists, and New Age shops. Fortunately, many outlets maintain a brisk mail-order business, so you need never be without an ingredient you seek.

By the way, "standard" strengths of ingredients (like the various oils) are what I use. And when a "capsule of vitamin E" is referred to, it is the 400 I.U. size. (An eighth of a tablespoon of wheat germ oil can always be substituted for the vitamin E in a capsule.)

Finally, begin to do a little experimenting of your own; and once you have found what your hair and scalp seem to respond best to, you may want to keep in mind that particular ingredients are more appropriate for dry or damaged hair, others for oily and/or coarse hair:

For Dry Hair	For Oily Hair
Rose Petals	Marigolds
Eucalyptus	Herbal Vinegar
Glycerine	Nettles
Honey	Wheat Germ Oil
Egg Yolk	Yogurt

NOW BACK TO THE SCALP

One of the things I do suggest is to **protect your scalp by diluting your shampoo**. (Would you wash your face with a harsh, full-strength detergent every day?) Instructions are given in the next chapter.

MOISTURIZING AND TONING YOUR SCALP

The moisturizing and toning of your scalp is also a critical part of keeping it healthy. It is *not the same as conditioning your hair*, which is basically a smoothing, protective process for the hair shaft.

Here is a good basic moisturizer for the scalp:

Scalp Moisturizer

1 tablespoon coconut oil	1 tablespoon natural bran
1 tablespoon nettles	2 capsules vitamin E (400 I.U. each)

Process in blender for 30 seconds. Massage into hair. Leave on 10 minutes and then wash out with two or more latherings of diluted shampoo.

Sometimes the scalp doesn't need conditioning as much as it needs toning (just as coarse, oily skin does). Here are two "tonics" for drab, oily hair that comes from overactive sebaceous glands in the scalp. As they tone, they will add highlights and shine. (Note: These tonics should *not* be used on colored hair.)

Tonic for Natural Blond Hair

1 cup apple cider vinegar	2 ounces marigold petals
Juice of 1 lemon	1 ounce witch hazel

1 ounce nettles	3 cups water
2 ounces chamomile	

Bring apple cider vinegar and lemon to a boil in a small glass or enamel pan. Add herbs and take the "tonic" off the heat. Add witch hazel. Steep for 5 minutes and then add water to stop process. Strain and let cool. Use whole amount--1 cup at a time--rinsing the tonic through your hair and then massaging it into the scalp. Leave on 5 minutes and rinse with clear water before styling.

You can also use this preparation as a "refresher" when you comb and style. Just spritz it on.

Tonic for Natural Brunette Hair

As above, but substitute sage and rosemary for chamomile and marigold, and orange juice for the lemon juice. Follow above directions for use.

SCALP PROBLEMS

Scalp problems not only affect the way your head feels. they also affect the way your hair looks. And although most scalp problems are rather easily solved with a little attention to your skin's particular needs, some can compromise not only your hair's beauty, but its very life.

Most scalp problems are caused by too much or too little: **too much sun, too much heat, too much brushing, too much processing** (all resulting in dryness or irritation), **too much conditioning** (which can leave a gluey residue on the scalp, preventing the skin from breathing and causing irritation and itching), and the use of **too many styling aids** (gels, mousses, sprays, and so on); conversely, there's **too little washing** (itching, debris on the scalp, dandruff), **too little moisturizing of the scalp** (again, important to distinguish from conditioning the hair), and **too little stimulation of the scalp** (preferably by massage rather than brushing). Furthermore, many people suffer from a contact dermatitis that masquerades as dandruff from **allergic reactions** to their shampoo (often because it is used in much too concentrated a form), their conditioner, or those aforementioned styling aids. People with sensitive skin may also get this from detergent-washed clothes that are rinsed inadequately.

Basic scalp problems should be treated daily until a noticeable change occurs, then twice a week until there is a definite change. After that, experiment with other remedies to see how the hair and scalp react.

DANDRUFF

Real dandruff, which is a fungus infection-a sort of athlete's foot of the head--can be serious as well as unsightly. It can spread (to the eyebrows, for instance) if it is not taken care of. It almost always calls for a doctor's attention if it does not immediately respond to an over-the-counter preparation.

Be aware that one of the risks of self-treatment for dandruff is the exacerbation of a dry-scalp condition from using a medicated product.

TREATING DRY SPOTS

*Y*ou can help nature along with the **"wonder vitamin": E**. It's great for spot-treating dryness. Simply puncture a 400 I.U. capsule and rub the oil (you can substitute wheat germ oil) into any dry spots before going to bed. Leave on until morning, then wash it out in the course of your regular shampoo.

When your whole scalp is dry, or has been abused by sun, swimming, perms, or coloring, you might want to try this heavy-duty treatment:

The Vitamin E Cure

Puncture one 400 I.U. vitamin E capsule and squeeze contents into a small cup. Add 3 tablespoons of avocado or sunflower oil. Mix well and comb through hair.

Wearing rubber gloves, soak an old towel in hot water. Wring it out and then wrap it, still steaming, around your head. Leave the towel on until it cools. Repeat wrap and steam 7-10 times. With diluted shampoo, shampoo hair 3-4 times to get rid of all the oil.

THE SCALP MASSAGE

By now you know that **I consider scalp massage the single most important thing you can do on a regular basis--at home, on your own time--for your hair.**

As an avid daily practitioner of yogic scalp massage for over sixteen years, I am completely convinced of its benefits--either as an addition to any other exercise you do or by itself, as part of your hair care routine.

Massage encourages hair growth by stimulating the scalp's rich blood supply and helping to flush away metabolic waste. Moreover, massage supports the natural process of hair fallout in a process not unlike gentle skin exfoliation, which keeps skin looking bright and fresh rather than dull and grayed.

Finally, there is the pleasure and calming effect of the massage itself--sort of a workout for the head. (It's also good for the hands, arms, and shoulders. You'll feel that the muscles have tightened pleasantly after a good head workout.) Massage is a wonderful relaxer and stress reducer and, if you do it right, has all the benefits of a minimeditation.

THE TECHNIQUE

It is not hard to do this sort of massage, but the technique can take a little time to learn. You will want to remember to *use the pads of the fingers*, keep the hand spread out starfish style, and maintain a constant pressure. It is also important to get your fingers as much on the scalp *itself* as you can. Working backward--from the nape of the neck up against the direction of hair growth--will help you to get under the hair and lift it as you go.

This massage can be done before washing or after. If you do it after, with your hair still damp, you will be amazed at how effective it is in putting body into your drying hair. Be sure you are seated, to maximize the relaxation effects.

- Just at the start, keep your fingers gathered and place them at the base of the neck, with the fingers and thumb of each hand "pinching" the pair of muscle cords on the back of the neck. Begin with light pressure and a kneading motion on these cords. Do this for about thirty seconds or until you feel an opening-up sensation.

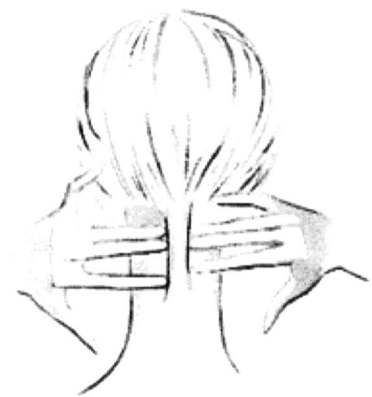

- Move the fingers slowly toward the crown of the head, making little circles as you go. These little circles should not "scrub" the scalp. Rather, if you have the right pressure, the scalp will move under your fingers--and over the skull bone--which is the effect you want to achieve. As you do this, allow the hand to spread so that the thumbs stay just behind the ears (in that soft spot) as the fingers advance toward the crown. The trip from base of the neck to the crown should take about a minute. Relax and enjoy it; don't hurry. You should begin to feel a tingling.

- You can press a little harder now, as you move your *thumbs* over your ears toward your temples, keeping the *fingers* squarely on the crown. You will want to move your thumbs in a slight zigzag pattern to make sure you have covered the sides of the head. This part of the trip takes about thirty seconds.

- When your thumbs are on your temples, begin to move your fingertips over the top of the head, toward your front hairline. (You may need to push up under the hair with your fingers to get directly on the scalp as you are moving in the direction of the forward growth.) You should take a full thirty seconds to get to the hairline; once there, make gentler circles (once again with your fingers bunched) all around the periphery of the hairline for one minute. Be careful not to scrub--especially here. Take your time and lift the hair from the hairline.
- Now put your head between your knees and, placing the very tips of the fingers on the scalp (starting at the front hairline), lift your fingers through the hair all over your head to detangle and to urge out any dead hairs that are ready to fall. When you have done this to top, sides, and back, sit back up slowly and then rest--with your eyes closed--for one minute. Try to keep your mind clear by focusing on how your scalp feels.

- Finally, plant the fingers firmly on the scalp in the forward position (thumbs on temples, fingers splayed over the top of the head), and start a back-and-forth vibration of the scalp over the skull. Move your fingers straight over the back of your head, using the thumbs as a fulcrum and only allowing them to move toward the back of the head as the fingers descend once more to the nape of the neck. Finish off with a few seconds of kneading the back of the neck, then quickly tap once all over the head with the very tips of the fingers, so that the touch feels like gentle rain.

- Smooth your index and middle fingers a couple of times over your forehead, from the center out, and then draw them over the eyebrows twice, to release any tension in the face.
- Sit with your eyes closed and your hands folded in your lap, this time for two minutes. Once more, concentrate on the sensation of your scalp and face.

This is the best ten-minute restorative I know of...and it's wonderful for your hair.

CHAPTER 3

Cleaning Your Hair

Shampooing seems like it ought to be the simplest of all hair procedures. It isn't. Most of my clients really *don't* know all they should about how or when to wash their hair...or with what.

WASH DAILY

It has been my observation over the years that **daily shampooing is not only acceptable; it is advisable**. It is healthiest for the hair and scalp for two reasons. First, the hair itself--especially in the city--gets dusty and dirty. (Just look at your windowsill on a warm day after the window has been open for some hours, and you'll have a good idea of what has been deposited on your head--and in your hair.) Moreover, the same substances that make conditioning agents so effective in smoothing and protecting the hair shaft (waxes, silicon compounds, oils) are like magnets for debris in the air. In all likelihood, your hair needs to be cleaned of this junk every day.

Second, shampooing cleans the scalp, flushing it of oil and other surface products that have been shed--like dead cells--that can block its "breathing" and interfere with new hair growth. It also works to discourage infections and--perhaps most important--stimulates the scalp so it can continue to renew itself.

So wash as often as you like...every day, if possible. But be careful how you do it.

SHAMPOO DILUTION: SAVE YOUR HAIR AND SAVE YOUR MONEY

What I recommend to most clients is exactly what is routinely done at almost all salons: **dilute your shampoo**. The typical commercial salon shampoo is much too concentrated to be used just as it comes from the bottle...and this is equally true of the brand-name shampoos you are likely to be using. These products are overly harsh--especially when used on a daily basis; they *are detergents*, after all. They are also likely to leave a shampoo buildup that makes hair dull, limp, and sticky; at the same time, they may quite literally be eating away at each hair's structure with chemical compounds. Diluted shampoo may not *entirely* solve some of the problems inherent in using such compounds daily on your hair, but it will certainly minimize them.

I like to dilute my shampoos in a one-to-seven ratio of shampoo to water. And if you are conscious of such things--and want to do all you can for your hair--dilute with softened or distilled water...or one of the floral or herbal waters you will learn how to make later in this chapter.

You will probably want to make a week's worth of shampoo at a time. There are lots of high-tech houseware stores around now that have great-looking dispensers in which to mix your concoctions.

An added bonus with diluted shampoos--and the accompanying diluted negative effects--is that you can feel better about washing your hair *more than* once a day...for those people who wash after exercise or more often than usual when the weather is hot or muggy.

Two soapings are required when using a diluted cleaning product... but you'll *still* be saving shampoo! And remember, even an expensive shampoo is much less pricey when it is cut seven to one.

CHOOSING A SHAMPOO

I can't pretend to be happy with the products I see on store shelves. I avoid them myself and can rarely find one to recommend. My frustration with the quality of the products I found commercially available for cleaning hair was a strong impetus to the development of the Fleuremedy line of natural hair care products, which are based on the finest herbal and floral extracts and the fewest F.D.A.-approved chemical preservatives consistent with stabilization of the inherently unstable ingredients (to maintain shelf life). It is primarily these preservatives and stabilizers in other commercial preparations (as well as the artificial coloring and fragrances) to which I object. They can do great damage to hair and scalp.

But Fleuremedy isn't always available, and it is impractical to *make* an effective shampoo. (Don't use bar soap! It leaves curds in the hair and is drying.) So where do you go for shampoo and other personal-care products when you want to avoid some of the nasty stuff in the mass-produced variety?

I always feel fairly confident sending clients to their local health food stores for shampoo. Formulas vary, but you can learn a lot by reading labels. Don't be afraid to ask questions of the people who run the store; most are knowledgeable and anxious to help you educate yourself. Established lines have good quality control and many more natural ingredients than "commercial" products. I don't know about you, but I would always rather use the more natural product. (I'm sure you will agree that it is at least disconcerting to read "methylchloroisothiazolinone" on the label.) A good rule of thumb is to choose the product with the fewest chemical-sounding names and the *most* ingredients that sound comprehensible and/or familiar, like "oil of jojoba." Something you do want to **stay away from** in any product you use on your hair is **alcohol**. Although not frequently found in shampoo, it *is* a common ingredient of hair-grooming products like gels and mousses and can be found even in conditioners--a most unlikely place for something so drying.

Some ingredient benefits you might want to keep in mind when you are shampoo shopping: jojoba is good for dry hair; protein-enriched shampoos with milk, egg, or beer help with the reproteinization of damaged hair; and shampoos with henna, a natural vegetable product--and an ancient treatment technique--which coats the hair (see [Chapter 10](#) for more about henna), will add body.

Some product lines I particularly like are Orjene, Weleda, Rainbow, and Schiff. You can find these in health food stores and catalogs.

SHAMPOO FATIGUE

Opinions vary as to whether a person should switch periodically from one shampoo to another. Some people say that shampoo is shampoo, and you can use one over and over again with no fear of buildup or--conversely--loss of effectiveness.

I don't think it can hurt--and it may help--to consider a switch every six months or to rotate regularly among two or three brands you particularly like.

PROPER SHAMPOO TECHNIQUE

So how do you wash your hair? First, **make sure you use the right shampoo and dilute it in the seven-to-one ratio** I already mentioned. Next, **be certain to wet your hair thoroughly** so that the shampoo "spreads" quickly and cleans rather than builds up in globs. This is important.

When you are ready to shampoo, apply the preparation you will use to the temples first (this often ignored area can get flaky; it also helps you to move the shampoo up with the blood flow), then to the front, then to the back and crown. If you feel you need more shampoo to get the right amount of lather, apply a little more behind the ears and above the back of the neck, then massage the shampoo upward once more. (Think how often in brushing, combing and smoothing you go in just the opposite direction!) Use the pads of the fingers to massage gently (keep your massage "progression" in mind) until the whole head is lathered.

Rinse (you can use regular tap water for this rinse; I suggest making your own herb or flower water--recipes to follow--for the final rinse) and repeat. But **this second time, once the lather has been worked up, use a widetoothed comb and start at the ends of the hair, working the comb through carefully.** You will start the stroke progressively closer and closer to the scalp as the hair begins to lather and detangle.

If you intend to use a conditioner after you wash, you can once again rinse with tap water. Otherwise, use the special rinse water you will have prepared.

THE RIGHT WAY TO RINSE

R**insing is the single most important part of your shampoo.**

There are two elements to a good rinse: the rinsing technique and what you rinse *with*.

First of all, good rinsing technique requires that you use enough water to accomplish the job. This sounds ridiculously self-evident, but at our salon we often find that when water is first run through a client's hair to wet it, residual suds appear. And one of the biggest dullers is soap left on the hair. So water, water, water...cascades of it. "Squeaky clean" is the standard that comes to mind.

The next important consideration is what you use to rinse *with*. And while I can--and will--give you some recipes for herb and flower waters that will at the very least make the last rinse a more aesthetically pleasing experience, you should know that **the composition of the**

basic tap water you use may affect the kind of "clean" your hair is getting.

THE WATER YOU RINSE --AND SHAMPOO--IN

*I*f your hair looks drab even after you have done your best for it, you should consider the possibility that the water you are washing in is hard. This means it contains dissolved minerals (iron, copper, and sulfur are some of the more common ones) that can not only dull your hair--and sometimes even *tint* it pinkish or greenish--but damage it, too. Dissolved minerals and other impurities can act on protein in the hair shaft to break it down and discolor it, leaving you with dry, dull, treated-looking hair that will be increasingly resistant to your attempts to make it look shiny and healthy.

If you *do* have hard water, my suggestion is to **make gallon jugs of softened water to use for shampooing and--just as important--rinsing.** You should notice an immediate improvement in the condition and look of your hair...especially in the winter. Use any good, water softening preparation and follow the directions; if it's good enough for your laundry, it's good enough for your hair.

An alternative to softened water is plain distilled water. You can buy distilled water in gallon jugs at any grocery store. It isn't expensive but can be an annoyance to lug home. Distilled water is distinguished by what is not in it rather than by what *is*.

By the way, some people think that a cold-water rinse helps to flatten out the hair's cuticle so it appears shinier. There is no real evidence that this is so, and it is my own belief that the warmer the rinse water, the more likely it is to carry off dissolved dirt, waxes, and other debris. If you are convinced of cool-water benefits, however, rinse completely with warm water first, then once again with cool.

HERBAL AND FLORAL WATERS

Best of all, in my opinion, is rinse water (and shampoo-mixing" water) that you have made yourself. Begin with softened tap water (or water you have softened yourself) or distilled water, then make yourself jugs of these special waters to use whenever you need them.

Following are some recipes; you may want to alternate among them, or you may find that a single one is best for your hair and scalp...or most pleasing to your sense of smell. This is also a recipe area that encourages your creativity: if there is any particular herb or flower for which you feel a special affinity, experiment with highly diluted "teas" made with your ingredient of choice: **simply brew as you would any tea, then add purified water.** (Try, for instance, a tea of birch bark and wood--it's a favorite with the Finns in their saunas.) You'll have a less satisfactory result with ordinary fragrance products because they are made with oils, alcohol, and stabilizers. Nothing beats an "essence" of your own creation.

Scented herbal waters give you the extra benefit of aromatherapy--naturally--as you wash and rinse your hair. They are a *real* pleasure to use.

Rose or Orange-Blossom Water

> If you don't choose to create your own "brew," you can make some lovely floral water with the small bottles of rosewater and orange-blossom water that can be bought in gourmet shops (they are used as flavoring in baked goods and drinks). Use the bottled preparation in a 1:20 dilution. This should be enough to leave just the gentlest hint of scent in the water.

Chamomile water is especially suitable for lighter hair shades and, if used in the summer (when there is subsequent sun exposure), will keep your hair bright looking.

Chamomile water should only be used every other day. It can also be used alone--*undiluted*--as a refreshing shampoo substitute in the summer.

Chamomile Water

> Steep 1/2 cup of dried chamomile flowers in 2 cups of boiling water. Let stand until cool. Strain off the flowers and dilute to fill a gallon jug.

Here's another basic, all-purpose rinse water that is especially good for shining up your hair if it has dimmed from overtreatment or too much indoor heat.

Gleam Rinse

Mix 1 part apple cider vinegar with 7 parts water. Store in a closed container.

CHAPTER 4

Conditioning Your Hair

Conditioning is another of those things that seems more obvious than it is. And while it is harder to do actual damage with the wrong conditioner, your hair can certainly end up looking bad.

First of all, it is important to distinguish between two kinds of conditioning: the kind you do in conjunction with shampooing to help repair minor damage and keep your hair looking shiny and healthy, and the "therapeutic" or "deep" conditioning for major problems that is usually done *before* washing so that the treatment substances can do their work and then be washed out. What is considered *everyday* conditioning is what I will discuss here (although **I am personally opposed to using a conditioner every day**); conditioning *treatments* will be dealt with in the next chapter.

SO WHAT DOES REGULAR CONDITIONING REALLY DO?

Considering the amount of money manufacturers spend touting their conditioning products, you would think unconditioned hair was some sort of disaster. I'm sure it will come as no surprise, however, to learn that conditioners are not the panacea advertisers would have you believe. What a conditioner does do, as I mentioned earlier, is simply to coat the shaft of the hair (usually with a waxy or silicon-derived substance) so that the cuticles lie flat and sleek rather than flaring out at all angles (which makes the hair seem dull, flyaway, and dry). It can also "stick together" frayed (split) ends. And conditioner can *protect* the cuticles--encase and/or help to smooth them--and consequently protect the hair shaft itself from damage...or further damage.

Conditioners have another advantage: they can lock in a certain amount of moisture--under the waxy coating--so that hair doesn't get parched from heat, sun, or dryness in the air. Rather than nourishing hair, therefore, it functions much as a leather reconditioner does, giving it a good waterproof protective coat so that the moisture it *does* contain isn't lost, and harsh factors in the environment (or in your styling habits) cannot do more harm.

WHEN TO CONDITION

I think it is fair to say that problems with conditioning come not from too little too late, but from too much too often. The fact is that while conditioners can consistently help the texture of processed and/or damaged hair--and they certainly make postwashing detangling easier--*normal healthy hair needs relatively infrequent conditioning*. Even damaged hair does not need it after every washing. **Two to three times a week is enough conditioning for anyone unless the hair is damaged at the roots.**

HOW TO CONDITION

*W*hen you *do* use a conditioner, make sure you use it properly. Conditioner is meant to be applied to the *hair*, not to the *scalp*, where it can clog pores, make you break out around the hairline, and leave a waxy residue on the skin. (For moisturizing your scalp, review Chapter 2.)

This means that once you have the small amount--about the size of a quarter--you intend to use in your hand, you must concentrate on getting it onto--and into--*the ends* of the hair...which is where it is almost always needed most. You should therefore start your conditioning at least halfway down the length of your hair and preferably confine it to the ends alone. Even if your goal is detangling, you will, I think, find it instructive to examine the knots in your hair: you will see it is really the *ends* that cause the tangles, rather than the middle of the strands of hair. Comb out will also go much more smoothly if you work from the ends up...something that is always done in a salon.

And remember, *conditioning cannot cure the problem of damaged hair; it can only lessen it.* The damage comes from the stripping and breaking of the cuticles and from fraying at the ends of the strands. It is this damage that allows hair to catch on itself, tangle, look dull, and feel coarse. The only *real* cure for damaged hair is to cut it, although there are a number of relatively therapeutic preparations (both commercial and--my preference, of course--homemade) that can make damaged hair look better and feel healthier until the damaged parts grow out enough to be trimmed off. (See Chapter 5, "Keeping Hair Shiny," for recipes.) This is also a good place to mention that having hair trimmed regularly can stave off further damage, as the chips and breaks and peeling of the cuticle can and will travel up the hair shaft unless they are removed.

DILUTE YOUR CONDITIONER, TOO

*J*ust as I recommend diluting shampoo, I recommend diluting your conditioner: **a ratio of one part conditioner to three parts water** (use your prepared water) is about right for most conditioners. When you have mixed your conditioners), be sure to shake them before use, as the water and other ingredients tend to separate.

I also advise using less conditioner than manufacturers suggest: you should probably **use as little as you can to get the results you want**. If you *do not* choose to dilute your conditioner, use *much* less than suggested: half a teaspoon is all you need for short hair, one teaspoon for medium lengths, and two teaspoons (at the most) for very long hair. If you feel you need further guidelines, or your conditioner is somehow unusual in its concentration or consistency, read the instructions on the bottle and then halve the suqgested amounts.

CHOOSING A CONDITIONER

I hope it is not too obvious to mention here that light conditioners are appropriate for oily or coarse hair-as well as for fine hair that gets limp looking--and that heavier conditioners are best for fine, frizzy, processed, or weather-damaged hair.

Some general advice: stay away from anything that sounds like a stew of chemicals. There are certain natural substances I look for in conditioners--among them jojoba oil, coconut oil, and lavender, rose, and cucumber extracts. These shouldn't hurt *anybody's* hair.

CREAM RINSES AND "INSTANT" CONDITIONERS

*T*hese products are essentially the same: water-based light conditioning that combs in or sprays onto hair after shampooing to ease comb-out and help protect against damage associated with brushing or blow-drying. Because most do not contain the waxy elements that can build up with other conditioning formulas, they wash out completely in the next shampoo.

SHAMPOO/CONDITIONER COMBINATIONS

One of the newer "technological advances" is the blending of cleaner and conditioner in the same product. It is difficult for most people to imagine how one product could simultaneously accomplish what seems like two contradictory processes. It is just as hard for me to imagine they do both equally well. There are plenty of adequate to good products that either clean or condition, so stick with the specialists.

NATURAL REMEDY EVERYDAY CONDITIONERS

Because, as I said, I don't think of healthy, normal hair needing much in the way of a conditioner unless it has been abused in some way, I offer three basic conditioners for dry, oily, and "compromised" hair that has been permed or colored.

Dry hair can be lackluster, brittle, look grayed and "old". Try this recipe to give it substance, help lift its spirits.

Dry Hair Conditioner

2 tablespoons coconut oil

1 tablespoon avocado oil

1 teaspoon crushed dried rose petals (optional)

1 tablespoon rosemary oil

2 capsules vitamin
E (400 I.U. each)

Shake or mix together until well blended. Apply and leave on 10 minutes. Wash out with diluted shampoo. Rinse with herb or flower water.

Oily hair can always use a pick-me-up that doesn't leave it stripped. This recipe will do just that...with the added benefit of being a brightener.

Oily Hair Conditioner

2 tablespoons wheat germ oil	Juice of one lemon (strain out any pulp)
1 tablespoon crushed nettles	1 tablespoon apple cider vinegar

Massage into hair and scalp. Leave on 5 minutes. Wash out with 2-3 sudsings of diluted shampoo, and rinse carefully.

We all know what can happen to overtreated hair. This preparation staves off that "fried" look and helps your hair to recover. The special ingredients here are the flowers.

For Treated Hair (Colored and/or Permed)

2 tablespoons coconut oil	2 capsules vitamin E (400 I.U. each)
1 tablespoon avocado oil	1 tablespoon crushed marigolds
1 tablespoon virgin olive oil	1 tablespoon rose petals

Process for 30 seconds in blender. Leave on hair for 10 minutes. Wash out with 2-3 sudsings of diluted shampoo. Rinse thoroughly with herb or flower water.

CHAPTER 5

Keeping Hair Shiny

If you ask people what one quality they most seek in their own hair--or notice first in someone else's--they are likely to say "shine." This makes good intuitive sense to me and is consistent with my convictions about health and beauty. As I said at the beginning of this section, healthy hair is beautiful hair. And beautiful hair is shiny...literally reflecting its state of health.

So in this chapter I want to discuss the getting and keeping of the quality that for many of us *defines* beautiful hair: shine. We've already been through doing what we can to improve the *health* of the hair; now I want to talk about enhancing its natural beauty...no matter what sort of problems you may have started with.

DRABNESS

Dryness is probably the most common cause of dulled hair... although you should be clear that dry *hair* may very well not mean dry *scalp*. (Review the last couple of chapters for distinctions.) You should also determine whether your hair is naturally dry and/or fragile (very fine and curly, for instance, or "older"), or whether you have inflicted the "dry" condition on it...which is much more likely. Use your common sense, or ask your hairdresser.

Some cases of dryness require a real arsenal of moisturizers and conditioners; I will talk about this shortly. When you find yourself with a case of the hair blahs, and need a little brightness pickup without getting involved with the replacement of oils, try this light herbal rinse to give dry hair sheen:

Herbal Treatment for Dry Hair

2 teaspoons nettles   2 teaspoons dill
2 teaspoons rosemary

Steep herbs in 1 pint of hot boiled water for half an hour. Strain and let cool. Use as a final rinse.

FRIZZ

*T*here are people who think they were born with frizzy hair, but **"frizz" is really breakage** that occurs in curly hair (whether that curl is natural or processed in). It must be cut off to be "cured."

Curly-haired people tend to be very rough on their hair in an attempt to wrestle it into manageability...and the curlier it is, the more they punish it for being so recalcitrant (and perhaps for being a subtle reminder of all the things in our lives that are not susceptible to our will). All this does is break it further...which makes it harder to manage--even to get a comb through...which breaks it further...and on and on.

SPLIT ENDS

*S*plit ends are another "drabber" to which no one is immune; in fact, they occur at least as frequently in straight hair (where they are more noticeable) as in curly hair. Again, the only real cure is cutting...and careful attention to avoiding a recurrence.

Split ends are simply the breaking apart--the "splitting"-of the hair sheath from the ends toward the scalp. Most likely to occur because of overbrushing (which causes static electricity) or "tearing" with a comb, especially when the hair is wet, split ends are vulnerable to dryness and damage from sun, heat, and processing. (This is one of the reasons I am so convinced of the benefits of finger-drying, detailed in Chapter 7.)

Paint this glossing formula on those ends before shampooing to bring back the well-nourished gleam:

Paintbrush Hair Glosser

1 tablespoon almond oil	2 drops of your favorite fragrance (optional)
1 tablespoon avocado oil	½ cup coconut oil

Mix well in a wide-mouthed jar. Using a 1-inch-wide paintbrush, apply to ends of hair. Leave on for 1 hour before washing out.

LOSING SHINE WITH AGE

Hair tends to become less shiny as we age, getting coarser (with the gray), drier (at the scalp), and less abundant. It grows more slowly, and the shafts of hair may come in with a less-than-perfect sheath of cuticles. Some of this can be avoided: too many people pay inadequate attention to nutrition as they age and fail to get enough exercise; this inevitably shows up in the condition of the hair.

There is another source of drabness in more mature hair: older women tend to do more to their hair. They are less likely to wear it in a style that moves freely, to touch it, to run their fingers through it, and to brush it (all habits that stimulate the scalp). And with the hairdos they are more likely to choose, they color and perm more often and stress hair with setting lotions and rollers, hair dryers (usually of the old helmet type), and lacquer-y sprays.

Try this restorative for coarse, dry, "older" hair:

The Mayonnaise Proteinizing Treatment

Using a fork, whip together 2-3 tablespoons of mayonnaise and two egg yolks. Comb through hair.

Cover with a shower cap and leave on for 2 hours or more; then shampoo out. (This will take at least 2-3 washings with diluted shampoo.)

Rinse with "Gleam Rinse" (see Part 4).

TREATING DAMAGED HAIR

Here is my heavy-duty remedy for hair that is really suffering--that has had just about everything done to it and looks it. The "Hair Drink" will clean, proteinize, and condition dry, processed, abused hair. As good for the scalp itself as for the hair shaft and root, it is made in a blender and will keep in the refrigerator for up to one week.

The Hair Drink

2 cups skim milk	1 tablespoon lecithin
2 tablespoons natural bran	2 capsules wheat germ oil (400 I.U. each)
1 tablespoon wheat germ	1 egg yolk

Put all ingredients into a blender and blend until smooth. Pour onto hair before shampooing, leave on for 10 minutes (this is a good time for a massage), then shampoo out 3 times.

Rinse with "Gleam Rinse."

HOT-PAKS

*T*here are basically two types of heavy-duty conditioners: those you apply and then wash out after giving them some time to do their work, like the "Hair Drink," and those that require heat and moisture to do their best for you.

Read the directions carefully on any commercial preparation as to which you should do, but **for any of my recipes, you can always use the hot-pak method if you have the time** and would like to treat yourself and your hair.

At home you need nothing more than a couple of old towels, a basin of very hot water (wear rubber gloves to squeeze out the towels), and some time, Although heating caps are available commercially, I don't recommend them; they produce a dry heat that doesn't do nearly as much for your hair as the steam from the towels you have soaked yourself. (Steam from hot-water-soaked towels softens the outer layers of the hair and encourages maximum penetration of the treatment into the hair shaft. This is much like what you must do to restore leather--first moisturize it and then condition/protect it.)

One of the great side benefits of an herbal hot-pak, again, is the accompanying spirit-lifting aromatherapy-*much* more intense than is possible with a nonheat remedy application.

Here are the **basic steps for a good hot-pak**:

1

Mix ingredients carefully and thoroughly.

2

Massage preparation well into wet hair and scalp.

3

Use alternating clean towels, letting one soak in hot water while the other is on your head.

4

Allow three to five minutes on the head for each towel--after that, it will be too cool to do any good.

5

Repeat application four to six times.

6

After towel treatment, put on shower cap and relax for ten minutes, allowing conditioner to set.

7

Wash out completely with diluted shampoo.

Here is a good, general-purpose hot-pak conditioner to replenish oils and help repair frizzed and split ends:

Richard Stein's Hot-Pak

3 tablespoons apricot oil	3 tablespoons eucalyptus oil
3 tablespoons avocado oil	1 tablespoon nettles

1 egg yolk

Put into blender and process until smooth. Massage into hair and then follow with hot-paks. Leave on at least 15 minutes, then wash and rinse out well.

May be used as often as once a week.

BRUSHING

Don't believe it: one hundred strokes of the brush a night can do a lot more harm than good. Three times a week is plenty...and for delicate hair, even that may well be too much.

The old notion that brushing makes hair glossy undoubtedly came from the beneficial effects of dust removal in long hair that was usually washed only once a week (if that) and in the distribution of natural oils from the scalp in the hair. In this quarter of the twentieth century, however, with shorter, more casual styles and frequent washing, brushing has lost much of the value it once had. Its major benefit--scalp stimulation--is, in fact, better served by massage, which does everything brushing does without the attendant risk of damage.

WHEN TO BRUSH... IF YOU MUST

*I*f--and when--you do brush your hair, **don't do it when it's wet**. Best to use a wide-toothed comb.

Instead, use a conditioner on your hair (if necessary) and then detangle it with your fingers (another good time to get in a little scalp massage). If your hair tangles badly when it's clean, very likely it's damaged and needs remedial care ... which means a trim, at least.

Avoid brushing your (dry) hair in arid, moisture leaching environments... like the dead of winter in an overheated house or under the noon sun in Palm Springs. The inevitable static electricity can ruin your styling and damage the hair shaft. A good time to brush is after a bath, when your hair has been "moisturized" by the ambient water carried in warm, humid air.

HOW TO BRUSH... WHEN YOU DO

*S*tart with that gentle detangling with fingers, whether your hair is wet or dry. (You might want to do this with your head hung upside down.) *Don't "brush out" the knots.*

Whether you begin right side up or upside down, brush the underneath layers first, either starting at the back of the neck (upside down) or (right side up) by lifting longer hair from the crown and brushing back and sides separately. Use your massage pattern of working toward the crown and top of the head, remembering that it is most often the sides and lower half of the back of the head that get short shrift. The *final* thing to do is brush all the way from the forehead to the nape of the neck, gently but firmly.

Because brushing does do most to distribute the oils of the scalp to the hair, people with dry hair should brush longer than those with oily hair, who ought to confine themselves to a good detangling and smoothing. People who also have a dry scalp, however, must be cautious about irritating delicate skin with too vigorous a brushing--which can lead to soreness and even bleeding.

THE BEST USE OF A BRUSH: STYLING

Brushes are of most use in finishing off a hairstyle, and I almost always use one when I blow-dry hair. Round brushes that serve as roller substitutes are especially helpful. If used correctly, they will not damage hair. (See Chapter 7 for blow-dry instructions.)

A regular brush can give body to a last-minute styling effort and should be saved for that. A favorite trick of mine when I do photoshoots is to blow-dry (or set) into the general shape, arrange the hair with my fingers, and then let the "creation" sit for a couple of minutes. I wait to brush until just before the model goes on. Those few minutes of rest do wonders for the final effect.

CHOOSING THE RIGHT BRUSH

Natural-bristle brushes are the kind that usually come to mind when you think "brush" and for which you can spend an enormous amount of money. They may be good for the ego (and usually feel best on the scalp) but don't really do that much; they are less versatile than the more specialized brushes you may want to switch to if and when you drop regular brushing from your hair-care regimen in favor of massage.

Don't use a natural-bristle brush for detangling wet hair; for that matter, these brushes can be at least as damaging to dry hair because of the static electricity they generate (which roughs up cuticles). Reserve them for impressing your friends and for finishing touches during styling.

Nylon brushes (such as the Denman brush) are extremely useful for detangling and for serious styling jobs like back-brushing. However, I do recommend *treating* this kind of brush by immersing it in very hot (not boiling) water. This will soften the ends of the bristles enough so that they will neither scratch your scalp nor break your hair, and that little bit of resilience will give you more control during styling. (This is a good idea for your natural-bristle brush as well. Just before the first use, soak it in hot water and shake it out; it will be kinder to your scalp *and* hair.)

Round brushes are used for styling with a blow-dryer (they work like rollers) and come in all sizes, from half an inch to four inches in diameter. A professional is likely to have a selection on hand; however, you will want to have only the size(s) you need for your hairstyle. I will explain how to use this kind of brush for styling in a later chapter.

PART 3

SHAPING UP–
Cutting and Styling

CHAPTER 6

Getting The Cut You Want

Because I have such respect for hair and its inherent beauty, I am very cautious about how I cut. (I often think that some hairdressers see hair as the enemy, to be tamed and shamed.) I really do work almost millimeter by millimeter, experimenting, adjusting, seeing how this entity--your hair--responds to a loss of weight here, more movement there, a cowlick on top. It is wonderful to see the shape *emerge* from a head of hair, and, although I am hardly Michelangelo, I get a taste of that feeling of artistic accomplishment that he talked about experiencing when he was able to "liberate" form from stone.

When I cut hair, therefore, I am hardly dealing only with what is growing on someone's head. Instead, I must keep in mind the sum total of my experience of the person I am cutting--height, weight, life-style, face shape, bone structure, hair quality, condition, color, and texture. And when I work with a woman (because I do cut men's hair, too), I must be just that much *more* sensitive and careful: there are more variables.

For me, cutting a woman's hair is not too far removed from making up her face. I must keep the same things in mind--natural coloring and how to enhance it, how to highlight beautiful cranial and facial structure and direct attention away from any less-than-perfect feature, how to work with the texture of the hair, how to play down the effects of aging, and how to bring the whole presentation into focus through attention to proportion and balance.

WHAT TO LOOK FOR IN A GOOD CUT

- **A good cut is highly individual**--that is, it shouldn't work on *anybody* else as well as it works on *you*.
- **A good cut never imposes the stylist's aesthetic.** Rather, it reflects you and adapts itself to you according to who you are and what your hair is like.
- **A good cut should virtually style itself** between salon visits (which shouldn't have to be closer together than every six weeks...unless your hair grows incredibly fast).
- **A good cut gives you choice and variety** so that it accommodates all the lives you lead--from very casual/drip dry to a more elaborate, formal, or stylized look for special occasions and evening. (See the Afterword: "Celebrating Your Hair.") With a good cut you should also be able to part your hair in more than one place for exactly this flexibility.
- **A good cut should look great without pins, sprays, teasing, and goop.** (A blow dryer is one aid that I don't love...but don't mind terribly, either.) You can, of course, use any of these styling aids when you want a special effect; you just shouldn't *have* to use them routinely to keep your hair looking good.
- **A good cut is an exact cut.** There is no room for sloppiness or approximation in a cut that must maintain itself.

- **A good cut is easy to maintain** because it is realistic about your hair's texture and thickness. If a haircut is functional, it is also beautiful.

HOW TO TELL WHETHER YOUR CUT IS GOOD

It's easy for hair to look good in the salon. But you can't tell whether you have a *really* good cut until after you leave the salon, get home, live with the new style for a couple of days, and then--this is the acid test--wash it and see if it falls into place. The cut that was spectacular in the salon may be unrecognizable when it is left to fend for itself, away from a solicitous hairdresser's ministrations.

Here are **five ways to check out your haircut**. (Your hairdresser should be doing the same five things while s/he cuts.)

AFTER YOU WASH YOUR HAIR:

1

While it is still wet, check the layering...if your hair is layered. If you look at the back and sides with a mirror, you will be able to see if the layering is even.

2

Take hold of the two strips of hair closest to your face on either side of it and pull them toward the chin. You can then see if they are the same length.

3

Part your hair from either side and then down the middle. Hair should fall into line regardless of where it is parted. There shouldn't be any "rogue" strands.

4

Let your hair dry naturally, pulling it from roots to ends to encourage the shape to return. (Do this gently at first, and then more vigorously.) Push it into place with your fingers. The line should fall in easily.

5

Grab your hair behind each ear and "scrunch" it. You should feel the same amount of bulk in each hand.

Finally, your style should be self-supporting, with closeness, volume, or height cut right in so that you don't have to create it with the aforementioned styling aids.

IF YOUR HAIR HASN'T BEEN CUT RIGHT

*D*on't just curse your luck and vow never to return to the person who committed the crime; you owe it to the salon and to yourself to go back and tell them you're not pleased. You can reasonably expect to have any mistake corrected.

There's always the chance they will make it worse rather than better. In that case there is little to do but let it grow out. (As serious as it may seem at the time, a sense of humor goes a long way toward repairing the disaster of a bad cut.) And next time go to a salon you have investigated more thoroughly.

WHEN DO YOU NEED TO HAVE YOUR HAIR CUT?

*I*n general, once you have had your hair cut sensitively, **your cut should last anywhere from six weeks to three months**, depending on the rate at which your hair grows. More important, it should keep the *shape* it was cut in; although hair does grow unevenly (especially in the back), a good hairdresser should allow for the "grow in." For some reason no one has ever been able to explain to me, it is my observation that the shape seems to come back strongly every three weeks or so in a kind of cycle.

When do you stop waiting for the shape to come back and get yourself to your hairdresser? When you find yourself fooling with your hair, having to comb, brush, or minister to it constantly to keep it looking fine. A push of the fingers and a shake of the head should be enough to do it, if it is not in need of another trim.

It is also important to **keep a close watch on the condition of your hair**. If your hair begins to look frayed, it needs to be cut before the damage spreads up the hair shaft. (This is not unlike plucking dead leaves off a plant to give the new growth a chance. You simply *must* cut damage off.) A change in the weather or the way you care for your hair (too much brushing in the winter, for instance), or exposure to sun or wind, can cause a lot of damage from one cut to the next. You may also have had your hair processed--either permed or colored--and need to cut off damage from the processing itself. (This damage may not be immediately obvious after it has been done.)

THINNING HAIR

There is one other situation in which frequent cutting is advisable, and that is when the hair is thinning. Although this is often thought of as an exclusively male problem, we are all susceptible to thinning hair as we age--especially at the crown. Hair that is thinning, then, needs special attention in two ways: cosmetically, to disguise the thinning and keep the hair "light" so that it appears to have more volume; and therapeutically, to keep the increasingly fragile hair from breaking and to encourage growth.

There is a fairly drastic technique I use...usually with men: if you look carefully at a hair growing in a thinning area (the hairline, for instance), you will see that the hair shaft gets more delicate looking about half an inch from the scalp. Cutting the hair just at that point--where the shaft itself gets thinner--seems to strengthen the hair, and I have been very pleased to note the apparent inhibition of the thinning process with this method.

LONGER VS. SHORTER HAIR

A drastic change in hairstyle or length is not irrevocable, of course, and the risk-taking involved is--*I* think--character building in itself. The worst that can happen is that you don't like the style and must wait for it to recover its length or shape. **Even slow-growing hair gains one-half inch a month, and fast-growing hair can gain almost an inch in the same amount of time.**

However, chances are you may even--like that favorite client of mine in part one--discover something wonderful about yourself with your new look, something positively transforming.

WHY LONG HAIR MIGHT NOT SHOW YOU AT YOUR BEST

*H*air that is longer than shoulder length is not very pretty in and of itself unless (1) you have a *great* deal of it; (2) it is superbly styled; and (3) it is very healthy. Long hair tends to get flattened by its own weight and look droopy and dead; natural waves are "pulled out" by the length. And all too often the hair is blunt cut, probably in some misguided commitment to the retention of every last inch, adding to its flabbiness. Hair like this, and especially hair that goes past the shoulder, doesn't move with the head and makes the whole face and body look less dynamic and alive.

As a result, the very advantage sought with long hair--the illusion of volume, of lots of bouncy, shiny hair--is lost. And because a woman doesn't know where that elusive volume has *gone* to, she thinks she must grow her hair longer in search of it. Inevitably, the longer it gets, the worse it looks, the more it drags down the face--and body--and finally, the older it makes her seem.

VOLUME

*V*olume is a very contemporary notion. It gives longer hair dimension and interest and frames the face. Volume can also help to balance your whole look, offsetting heavy hips, thighs, or buttocks, or drawing attention up and away from a large bust or a general weight problem.

Ironically, this is precisely what most long hair *fails to* do, simply because, as it grows past the shoulder, it draws the eye downward, to the body, making a woman seem shorter and heavier. Long hair also interferes with the shoulder and collar line, softening that high horizontal line and in that softening "rounding" the whole body and making it seem dumpier. And if you like good clothes, you will find *their* impact dulled with hair that falls over the collar and shoulder area. (You never see models during a fashion show allowing their hair to interfere with the line of the designer garments. Runway models usually wear their hair short and sleek--or up and sleek--unless the designer is looking for a particular effect.)

CUTTING IN VOLUME

*T*here are a number of ways to achieve volume. I approve of three of them: cutting volume in, drying it in (which you can do with finger- or blow-drying), and-if your hair is very straight and/or fine-a perm or bodywave. What I *don't* approve of on a daily basis (unless you are going for a special, high-image look) is the manipulation of hair by means of setting, teasing, and sprays. It takes a lot of your valuable time, the look itself is passé, and it doesn't help your hair's health one bit.

SCULPTURE CUTTING

I do something I call "sculpture cutting," which requires following the hair's natural lines and cutting so that those lines--or waves--are expressed. Sculpture cutting is really a direct outgrowth of my interest in natural pattern and the organic "soul" of an object. This technique not only results in greater volume; it also gives the hair movement, expression, and life.

   Some of my clients have been astonished to find that their "straight" hair is actually quite wavy once those waves have been cut in. **Even if there are no waves per se, each head of hair has its own "movement"**: it *must*, as all hair grows in a circular pattern from the crown of the head. (Take a look at the crown of your head with the aid of a couple of mirrors. It will help you to understand why your hair does what it does.) The growth pattern may be so pronounced that hair on one side of the face grows directly away from it, while hair on the other side grows straight toward it. And the shorter your hair is, the more these growth patterns will determine the look of the final style, as there are fewer ways in which to disguise direction of growth or cowlicks...which are smaller whorls-sort of "hair whirlpools"--that can turn up anywhere on the head and can make a particular hairstyle impossible to maintain easily.

   Sculpture cutting is especially effective around the face, and it is here that the hairdresser must be most skillful in making his or her judgments about what must be done. A good, sensitive sculpture cut can light up a face, drop years, and set the tone for the rest of the head and body.

SHORTER HAIR

I say "shorter hair" in preference to "short hair" because hair need not be what is thought of as short to have all the *advantages* of short hair. In fact, a good, well-thought-out, medium-length haircut can give you both looks--the illusion of length and volume and the neatness and impression of cropped hair--with different stylings.

Almost no one--especially the busy people I deal with--has time anymore to contend with a weekly visit to the hairdresser. Women are on the go--they travel, work out, swim, and play sports regularly-and they need hair that complements their life-style, dries easily, and falls into place with a shake of the head and a lift of the fingers. They also need a cut that will look as good in the sixth week as in the first, so hair cannot be cut into a "style" but must be shaped with an eye to its organic whole. Everyone is impatient with having to fool with hair for one second more than necessary.

Short hair--even very short hair--is glamorous, and new....And shorter hair--with a good cut--is infinitely more versatile (to say nothing of being much easier to take care of) than longer hair.

It is also my sense that women are beginning to prefer the *look* of shorter hair. Shorter hair poses a constant challenge to reexpression; running fingers through hair rearranges it continuously. And recently as women have become more comfortable with their sexuality and their own bodies, they have *wanted* to express themselves in every area of their lives...and in every aspect of their looks. What's more--to be quite blunt--a modern lifestyle dictates that hair must look as good getting out of bed as it did getting in. A woman wants to be ready to go instantly...and always.

HOW SHORT IS SHORT?

*T*here is a certain amount of judgment to this, of course...but judgment is what you are paying your hairdresser *for*. S/he will have to decide whether a given length will work for your hair...and your face, and your body...and s/he will need your input to know about your life and what you need-and expect-from your hair.

Hair should be short enough to give your whole look some lift, but still long enough to be versatile. (My general rule is to keep it a little shorter than chin length, as this shows off the neck and face to advantage.) In many ways, shorter hair is almost like a fashion accessory: it usually makes a clearer statement, is more highly and/or individually styled, and is much more definitely "worn" than longer hair.

THE LONG-SHORT OPTION

*Y*es ma'am, you *can* have it both ways: it is entirely possible to have the *advantages* of short hair and the illusion of long.

There are two effective ways to do this:

1. Keep the back very short but leave the front, top, and sides long (an option that has been very popular in recent years).
2. Do just the opposite, cutting in waves and movement around the face for expressiveness and in the top for vitality and lift, while leaving the "body" of the hair long.

So you see you do have nearly endless options in juggling between long and short.

PROBLEMS IN CUTTING SHORT HAIR

A shorter cut will bring out your hairdresser's talent...or lack of it. Short hair is much more unforgiving, not only because there is less margin for error (a mistake will show up in direct proportion to how short the hair is), but because it means that the hairdresser must really *understand* your hair...understand the way it grows, understand its type (hair that is only wavy when it is long may be quite curly when it is short), and pay close attention to the shape of your face and your head. Whether the hair next to your face grows forward or backward becomes critical when it is only an inch long; cowlicks you never knew you had may suddenly appear when the weight that has kept them flat is cut off, or some asymmetry of hair growth may show up--one you were never aware of because you had enough hair to hide it.

TEXTURIZING

I personally think the old blunt cut looks hard and heavy; it's difficult to achieve the fullness most women seek with a cut that drags down and flattens hair so much. So one of my favorite tricks-one you may not be familiar with--is what is called "texturizing."

This cutting technique is used to vary the weight of the hair--to soften a look (especially at its edges) or to lighten it--**so that the ends are released and have more vitality**. It is achieved by thinning the lower portion of the hair (in some places only the very ends) almost strand by strand, feathering it.

This texture can always be smoothed back with a gel or mousse if you want a more classical or severe look, but for day-to-day wear, texturizing can give a real lift.

One of the current trends in hairstyling is contrasts in hair--contrasts of texture, length, even color. Texturizing can accomplish this kind of contrast as an integral element of the cut, so it is often the first thing I suggest for someone who really wants a new look. A little experimentation can pay off in some lovely--and often very interesting--effects.

UNDERCUTTING OR POINTING

*U*ndercutting is another method of making hair seem livelier and fuller than it is on its own: it creates an illusion of more body than the hair actually has by shortening the layers underneath--*under* the style that is seen-so that they support the top layers.

Undercutting involves snipping short points of hair near the root to hold the rest of the hair up and out. Obviously this has to be done very carefully, or you can look like the mice have been at you, but skillfully accomplished, it can make you look as if you have a lot more hair--and your *hair* has a lot more bounce--than you (or your hair) really do.

LAYERING

Layering is what they used to do to "thin" hair so that it was more manageable. (All it really succeeded in doing, I think, was to make it look scrappy growing out.)

Now layering is a highly refined technique for giving hair texture, versatility, and movement without the loss of a clean line. Layering solves problems that were once addressed with perms, because--when done on hair that has the least bit of body or wave--it delivers fullness and curves without damage and without grow-out.

Layering essentially creates tiers of hair around the shape of the head.

I give special attention to the problem of blending layers into each other so that the grow-out period is graceful, and the layers "reweave" themselves as they get longer. *This is different from sculpture cutting*, as it is primarily a volume and shaping technique rather than one that concerns itself with hair's line and wave.

FINE, LIMP HAIR

*P*robably half of all women classify their hair as fine and/or limp. (The other half sees *theirs* as too unruly.)

If you have tried everything in the way of cutting in some body and movement, and your hair still lies there as if it died three days ago, *it may be that the only cure is either a body wave for lift and volume or a real perm*--of the full head or just the crown, top, or front (which is where the hair is usually finest and flattest and where it may also be thinnest because it gets most abuse). Alternately, **you might consider waving just the undersections**, so that they can support the top layers of hair, which will remain relatively straight. **This technique is called root perming.**

Here are some other tricks you can use to cope with fine or limp hair:

- Make sure your hair is cut *with* the direction of growth: if it is thin and fine, it will lack the weight to cover and hold a reversal (trying to make hair that only grows forward sweep back from the forehead, for example); if it is thick and fine, you will be fighting to keep it in place all the time.
- Consider bangs. Fine hair looks its draggiest around the face, where it quickly graduates from limp to stringy. Bangs also help disguise

thinness on top, which is more noticeable if your hair is fine. You can always brush them back.

Make sure bangs are cut well into the temple and then graduated into the cheekbone.

- Avoid heavy conditioners, especially those containing balsam or cholesterol; they tend to weigh hair down.
- Finger-dry your hair if you are not blow-drying it. (I don't especially like blow-drying, but it *does* add volume.)
- Use mousse or gel at the *roots* of the hair when it's nearly dry to give it a little extra body.
- Rather than giving in to the temptation to have your hair blunt cut to "make it look fuller," have it texturized so that you take advantage of whatever body it *does* have.

CURLY HAIR

*M*ost people with curly hair don't seem to realize how lucky they really are; for some reason, they are least likely to want to accept their hair for what it is and live with its natural state.

There's a nasty rumor going around that curly hair is much easier to cut than straight hair because the curl will hide any mistakes. This may be true right after a cut, but just wait until the hair begins to grow in! Straight hair is much more forgiving during the grow-in period than curly hair, which can get terribly wild looking if the cut wasn't good to begin with. But the myth persists, and lots of curlies rarely get the kind of cut they deserve.

The biggest error made in cutting hair is to try to make it all one length; **curly hair should be layered**... and if it's just wavy, sculpture cut. Length must also be played off against degree of curl, so that the head comes out looking balanced both in length and curl.

LOOKING YOUNGER

*T*here is one thing I feel very confident of, it is this: after a woman first comes to me, she will leave my salon looking ten years younger...and ten years better.

There is no question in my mind that the most youthful look is a natural one...which means not trying to cover up signs of your age; you're not fooling anyone. And a hairstyle of your youth--or alternatively, one of those I think of as "old lady hair" (set, teased, and sprayed)-- doesn't serve you well, either.

LOOKING YOUR
(SLIGHTLY OLDER & WISER) BEST

*T*here is so much a woman can do to play down the effects of aging--on her hair *and* her facial features! All too often, however, she depends on heavy makeup, hair coloring, perms, and other artifice to give the impression of youth. (This reminds me of the hairpieces some balding men wear. People remark, "Gee, that's a great-looking hairpiece ... very natural," when the whole idea is not to notice it to begin with!)

Here are some of my principles for looking your best--no matter what your age.

- **Don't hide your hair's color.** Most graying hair is actually quite lovely. (I know, I know...but it *is*.) There are very few women who look *better* (with their changing complexion tones) in the darker, more "saturated" hair color they had before their hair faded- usually to gray. That change in color value is a natural concomitant of aging and is almost always much more flattering to you. As skin gets paler and sallower with age, intense hair color only makes you look tired and drawn.

    If you do color, allow some gray to remain to soften the effect. Or, if what you are not happy with is the *color* of the gray, have your hair rinsed to keep your gray lively looking.

- **Here's a rinse you can use regularly:**

Gray Hair Brightener

1 tablespoon chamomile flowers
1 tablespoon rosemary
1 cup boiling water

Steep herbs in water to make a tea. Let cool and strain.

Use after regular rinsing as a final rinse, and leave on the hair. Style as usual.

- **Think carefully before** fooling with your hair's texture with **a perm or body wave** if it is graying; you may end up with an effect--or color--you hadn't counted on. Don't forget that your gray hair will almost always be coarser--and sometimes curlier--than your nongray hair was, You may find, in fact, that your impossibly limp, fine hair is finally manageable--and even *fun*--now that you have some gray...and your hair has some body.

- **Keep your hair shorter.** Short hair is younger, more contemporary, and the movement around your face can do a good deal more than age creams to take off the years. Well-cut hair can also camouflage some of the effects of age...and a little visual interest around the face will draw attention up from the body--and especially the hips, where most older women collect their extra weight.

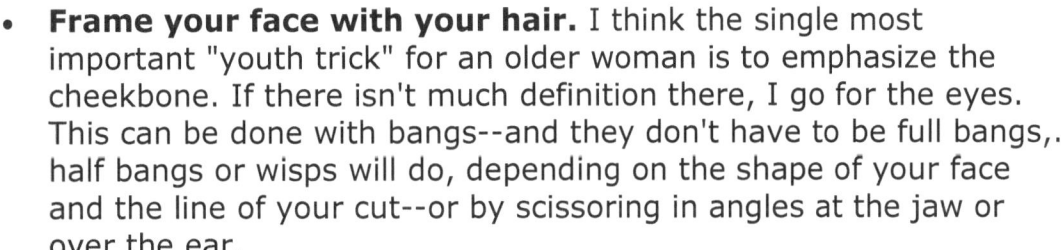

If you want to hang onto your *long* hair, at least wear it up and back so that it "lifts" the face (and body), drawing the eye up and away from the jaw line. And don't let it get too severe; it will look harsh, and *you* will look old.

- **Frame your face with your hair.** I think the single most important "youth trick" for an older woman is to emphasize the cheekbone. If there isn't much definition there, I go for the eyes. This can be done with bangs--and they don't have to be full bangs,. half bangs or wisps will do, depending on the shape of your face and the line of your cut--or by scissoring in angles at the jaw or over the ear.

Bangs have the added bonus of covering forehead lines.

CUTTING YOUR OWN HAIR

I'm all for self-sufficiency; as I said before, that is what this book is at least partly about.

However, it isn't so easy to be self-sufficient in the matter of cutting hair. It would be rare for *you* to be able to see what I see when I am cutting, and although a judicious trim here or there for a wisp that threatens to get out of hand is appropriate, I think it is best to leave the monthly or bimonthly hair overhauls to a professional.

What you *can* take care of yourself, however, are your bangs.

HOW TO TRIM YOUR OWN BANGS

I love bangs. They soften a face, add interest to good features, emphasize eyes and cheekbones, and look youthful. They can also shorten a long face or slim a wide one, depending on how they are cut.

Because there is so much bangs *can* do, they should initially be cut by a stylist so that s/he can decide whether they ought to be short or long; curved, straight, or tapered; full, half, or "wispy." Then, after they have been cut professionally, you can keep up with them at home (they will probably need to be looked after every two to three weeks) between salon appointments. I think it's a shame to have to run to your hairdresser just to have your bangs trimmed when you can do it so easily yourself...if you pay attention and are careful. Practice makes perfect.

When you get ready to trim, use the smallest-size (five inches--and *without* that little finger guard) haircutting scissors you can find, and make certain that they are sharp or they'll just push the hair around rather than cutting it cleanly. Always cut with the ring finger and thumb for the best dexterity.

After washing, towel-drying, and "pushing in" your hairstyle, size up your cutting needs a final time before taking the plunge (that first snip is always the hardest).

You won't want to be cutting off more than one-quarter inch when you do this. Occasionally someone will get carried away in the search for the perfect bang; then it's like cutting table legs: you never get them even, but they do get shorter and shorter. Remember, the length can vary just because of cowlicks, odd growth patterns, or the different ways your hair falls. Reassess when your hair is dry, and clean up any errant hairs.

CHAPTER 7

Styling the Natural Way- Hands-on Drying Methods

If your hair is cut properly, it should virtually style itself...and **if you know how to finger-dry, you can just wash and go**. I have outlined a *progressive program of drying/styling* that will let you choose just the right amount of involvement with your freshly washed hair to give you the results you want.

In general I am against using any styling aid that can damage hair...and the number-one common offender on my list is the injudiciously applied heat of a blow-dryer. Many people use this particular tool, and many people use it incorrectly. If you *must* blow-dry, learn how to do it with finger-combing, so that you can control the process and don't hurt your hair.

THE RIGHT WAY TO DRY YOUR HAIR

A good styling really begins the moment you start drying your hair after it has been washed. Resist the temptation to "scrub" your hair dry (something all of us tend to do...especially when we are in a hurry); instead, squeeze it gently in the folds of a thick towel. Don't use fabric softeners on your towels, by the way; it makes them soft and smell good, but it cuts down on their ability to absorb water.

When your hair has gone from wet to damp, you are ready to style it. With your fingers.

FINGER-DRYING

There are a few lucky people whose hair is "lively" enough to just wash and wear--it dries naturally, and the lines fall right in, with no loss of bounce and lightness. Even if this hasn't been true for you up until now, or if you haven't felt you wanted to try it, I still think you will find that, **with the right cut, finger-drying is all the styling you will need**.

I am very much against applying heat directly to the hair, and finger-drying is one way of helping hair to style itself without courting heat damage. Actually, finger-drying is related to the massage technique (see Chapter 2). The more you study your own head shape, the easier self-styling becomes.

HERE ARE THE STEPS TO A SUCCESSFUL FINGER-DRYING:

- Hang your head upside down and carefully pull fingers through the hair from root to end. Work from front to crown, then temples/sides to back. (Your finger positions should remind you of those you use for massage.) It is important to remember that you are *working through* your hair. Tease out any knots with your fingers, and *never pull!*
- When you have detangled your hair, give your head a gentle shake to encourage the hair to begin to "find" its shape.

- Flip your head up--and your hair back--and run your fingers through your hair once again from front to back (top first and then sides). You should do this even if you have bangs that will be pushed forward. You will, I promise you, begin to feel a sort of "lift" coming right from the roots of the hair.

- Depending on how thick and/or still wet your hair is, push fingers in toward the roots and lift hair away from the scalp with a little

shivery motion, encouraging it to dry in the air that you are shaking through it. Do this until the ends begin to dry.
- As soon as the ends are dry, you should pause to "press in" the shape of the style. Don't be afraid to use your fingers to mold a curve or direct the front or sides.

- Once you have shaped your hair, use fingers just at the roots to lift it once again away from the scalp. Try to do this without disturbing your shape, traveling from top front to crown and from temples to back. Be especially careful to get in under the hair behind the ears and to lift away from the back and sides of the head.

- You will probably want to go back to the crown to lift a final time, as this is where you are likely to be looking for extra height.
- Now let your hair finish drying naturally.

HERE'S HOW TO FINGER-COMB WITH A BLOW-DRYER:

- Start with hair that is almost (naturally) dry. Wet hair is more elastic and weaker and therefore easier to break.
- Use a blow-dryer with which you can direct the heat as much as possible. The better dryers come with a little baffle that can be fitted over the nozzle to give you a tighter "aim." The heat should be at medium high or high: this method uses short blasts of higher heat, which in the long run is, I think, less

damaging than going back over the hair again and again at a cooler temperature.
- Dry with your head upside down if it doesn't make you dizzy. Let gravity do some of your lifting work for you.
- Hold chunks of your hair by the ends, directing the blast at the roots for *no more than a couple of seconds* per chunk. This will leave the delicate, likely-to-fray ends to retain their natural curl and is kinder to them. Doing this all over your head will give you the basic lift.
- Now you will want to cover the whole head once more (you can go back to right side up). Beginning with the crown and using your fingers, lift the hair near the scalp and finish off the drying job. (Follow the same drying pattern you used for finger-drying, and don't forget to give special attention to the back; just because you can't see it doesn't mean it isn't as important--especially to balance the head.) If your fingers are down in the hair at the source of the heat, you won't overdry or burn the hair shaft.

- You will be surprised at how little drying there is left to do once the area near the scalp is dry. I prefer to leave the top layer just the littlest bit damp, to dry on its own. This gives a much more natural look to the hair and, as I said, protects those delicate ends. A light spritzing after your hair is dry will give the ends a little more finish and curl. (See "Hair Freshener" recipe at the end of this chapter.)

STYLING HAIR WITH A BLOW-DRYER

A blow-dryer can be used more actively, however--not just to bring out the best in your cut, but to actually "set" (or in some cases straighten) the hair. A blow-dryer used this way becomes in a sense a different tool and requires the partnership of a styling brush (usually a round one) to get the best results.

CURLING WITH A BLOW-DRYER

You can use a round brush (see the section on brushes in Chapter 5 for brush selection) like a large roller, directing the heat of the dryer right at it and then unrolling the brush gently, leaving each curl to cool while you go on to the next swatch of hair. (This cooling process is an important part of your set; don't touch the results until the hair shaft has cooled entirely. In fact, it's best to finish the whole head before testing the curls by pulling them out or brushing them into shape.)

You will of course need to choose a brush of the right diameter for *you*--smaller for tighter curls, larger for smooth curves. I prefer the larger brush in almost every case, but you might want to ask your hairdresser what s/he recommends.

When you set this way, be careful not to wrap the hair too tightly around the brush: it stretches when wet and then contracts as it dries, and if it is already tight around the brush, it will be stressed and may break.

It should also go without saying that you will need to be very careful about the amount of heat you apply, especially if you are not directing it at your scalp, which warns you when it is too hot. For this reason, I think it is best to be more conservative about the heat setting than you are when using the short hot bursts that are right for fingercombing.

TURNING THE ENDS

You may not want to set your whole head this way, but rather just give a curve to the bottom of the hair. This is called "turning the ends" and is one of the most time-honored uses of blow-dryer and brush. Skillful end turning can give a nice, smooth line to a midlength hairstyle.

To turn the ends, use a large-diameter brush. Catch just the ends of the hair (you may even want to pat the hair over the bristles if you are new to the technique) and then give a half twist to the brush.

Direct the heat at the ends and move the dryer back and forth over the length of the brush. You may find the hair slips slightly through the bristles. This is fine, as it helps the hair to curve as you are drying it. Just don't pull too hard!

Repeat for the ends of the hair all the way around the head. If you find that one part curves more than the rest, you can pull out the curl by reapplying heat as you pull the brush gently through that one spot.

USING A BLOW-DRYER TO STRAIGHTEN YOUR HAIR

I'm never sure I really understand why someone with curly hair would want to pull out all that dynamic movement (I'd certainly not do it to *myself!*, but there are people who for one reason or another want to use their blow-dryer to make their hair seem straight. So for them, here goes:

You use the heat of a blow-dryer to straighten hair in much the same way as one uses an iron to press cloth: the heat changes the character of a hair strand, and the pulling motion of the brush determines its new character. And just as you dampen clothes to encourage the best ironing job, so you leave your hair just a little damp to allow the heat to be most effective. (The same principle applies to nonheat drying, by the way. Some time try "ironing" a ribbon by wetting it and smoothing it onto some flat, nonporous surface--like a bathtub--and leaving it there to dry. This is like the old method of wrapping wet hair around the head and then allowing it to dry naturally to straighten it.)

HERE'S HOW TO STRAIGHTEN YOUR CURLY OR WAVY HAIR:

- Use the largest round brush you can find or a flat brush with a slight curve in its belly. This kind of drying can be especially hard on hair that tends to break easily and frizz at the ends anyway, so you will want to work as quickly as you can to smooth it and get it dry.
- If your hair is long or very curly, give a shot to the ends first by turning them just as you would if you were finishing straighter hair. (This helps to keep it from tangling as you work out from the scalp.)
- Start with the hair *underneath* at sides and back, then do the overlayers and top. Do the front last. This allows you to smooth the top layers after the others have been done. If the front dries while you are working on the rest of the hair, you can wet it with a little water spritz (preferably herbal or floral), or the "Hair Freshener" recipe at the end of this chapter.
- Start close to the scalp, hooking the brush into the hair near the root, and then very slowly pull it out toward the end. Play the hot air back and forth over the surface of hair exposed by the brush. The idea is to leave a smooth trail through the hair.
- You may find it most effective not to dry the hair completely the first time through, but to give yourself two "smoothing tracks"--one on top of the other--to ensure even drying. (A hot blast at the surface that is presented by the brush will dry only that surface. A second time through changes the presenting surface and gives you a more even dry.)
- Give yourself a last smoothing go-through, playing the heat lightly over the head and smoothing with the brush. (You can use one of

your regular or natural-bristle brushes for this job.) *Don't forget that your hair isn't done until it has cooled off.*
- If your hair is especially unruly, *spray hairspray on your palms -- not directly on the hair*--and smooth over the hair's surface. Or you can use pomade or brilliantine, which are discussed in the next chapter.
- *And...never try to hurry a job like this.* Blow-drying to straighten can take a considerable portion of your grooming time if it is done right. I *hate* the look that comes from haste or carelessness, where hair could pass for slabs of Brillo, shingled one patch over the other.

There is one really interesting effect you might want to try if you have wavy or curly hair, which can be achieved by blow-drying just the ends of your hair. This gives a sort of blunt-cut effect to hair that usually doesn't look that way and can be a nice change for someone who is always dealing with curls.

FRESHENING UP

I think it's always nice to have a bottle of hair freshener ready. You can use it to wet down for a between-wash styling, to cut static electricity in the winter, to perk up in the summer to revive curl, or just to freshen your mood.

Keep your hair freshener in the refrigerator.

Hair Freshener (Home Spritz)

In a spray bottle mix well the juice of half a lemon or half a grapefruit with 1 pint Perrier or Evian water.

Use when needed for a pickup.

CHAPTER 8

Styling with a Little Artifice

The easiest way is usually the best--providing you get the effect you want with your hair--which is why I love to dry and style the natural way, without depending on devices to do it. But sometimes--perhaps because you are feeling a little daring and experimental, or you want a more elaborate look for a special event, or you have simply given up trying to get your hair to do anything you consider acceptable--you want extra volume, body, height, or more curl or shape. Setting or perming (which includes the body wave--a light perm that changes the texture, body, and hold power of the hair) can do all these things, as well as giving you more flexibility in styling your hair.

As the word implies, "perms" are relatively permanent, lasting three to five months. Setting is temporary; as soon as you wet your hair, the curl will come out, if it hasn't already relaxed from humidity, or wind, or being slept on. How long a nonperm set lasts is determined by the texture, wave, and body (natural or artificial) already in your hair and how much abuse it is subjected to. Hair that already has body will hold a set much longer than naturally straight hair, as will a set that is teased and sprayed (although I *shudder* to think what it costs your hair); even a tight set tends to "slide out" of straight hair just in the course of an ordinary day. If you wash your hair every morning, this won't matter much, as the hair must be rewet to be reset. (You *can* do dry refreshers with hot rollers or a curling iron, but this is not very effective in holding a style.)

There are two basic ways to get a good set. The first--and oldest--is to set wet hair with curlers or roller or pipe cleaners or rags or clips. Then either let it dry naturally or "force-dry" it with some kind of hairdryer--hand held or the old helmet type. The second way is to set barely damp hair with a heating device: electric--or hot--rollers or a curling iron.

ELECTRIC SET OR WET SET?

*I*f you like the look that a roller set gives you, **I recommend the heating device method because I think that ordinary rollers damage the hair** in a number of ways: with the heat of prolonged forced-air drying, of course, but also because wet hair gets stretched around a roller (so the roller doesn't slip), and as the hair dries, it contracts and may break. I especially dislike those rollers with brushes in them because they tangle so badly in the hair, and women tend to yank them out--usually with some hair--in frustration.

By the way, whenever you are working with rollers or other curling devices--whatever the kind--be sure to unroll or undo them in the opposite direction you rolled them or did them so you don't tear your hair. A roller or clip should never be dragged out; it can't be considered free of your hair until it actually falls into your hand.

HEAT SETS

*Y*ou can get just as much body with electric rollers that are used *right* as you can with a wet set...and it's a whole lot faster. And although learning to use a curling iron is tricky, it can become a life saver--for touch-ups, for spot work (at the crown, for instance), and for those difficult little hairs around the hairline and neckline.

HOW TO USE ELECTRIC (HOT) ROLLERS

*H*air should be moist--not quite dry--when you use hot rollers (the idea is not to bake the curl in, but to coax it in). The heat of the roller should simply finish the drying process. If you are freshening a set, or setting dry, you will want to use either the "Hair Freshener" (the recipe at the end of the previous chapter) or a setting lotion--which can be commercial or homemade: **a good homemade setting lotion is beer mixed one to one with water**.

Your roller equipment will signal you when a roller is ready to be placed in the hair. Try not to let the rollers overheat, unless you are using them as a curling iron substitute. I personally prefer not to let a roller remain in the hair for more than two minutes, so **you should plan to start removing the first rollers before putting the last ones in**. In this way you can also get away with fewer rollers, as they can be reheated and reused.

For the most natural look, I place the rollers randomly rather than in strict rows, and I use relatively large sections of hair (1 1/2 to 2 1/2 inches): the smaller the section and the smaller the roller, the tighter the curl. This also helps discourage the roller marks that occur with more traditional sets. And try not to use a comb to part and set; instead, divide sections with your fingers.

Remember that you are not completely set until your hair has cooled as well as dried, so pull rollers out carefully--trying not to undo the curl-- and then **leave the curl alone until it is completely cool**.

When your set is finished and all your hair is cool, **finger-comb before brushing, combing, or teasing**, and then shake your head so you can see the shape. You may need to go back over a section, or you may decide you want a bit more fullness or height. Don't worry, the rest of the set will wait until you are finished...and when you're completely finished, *that's* when you'll want to do your styling. (See the next chapter, "Finishing Touches.")

CURLING IRONS

A curling iron can be especially useful for curling the short, fine hair around the face and neckline or for other spot curling at the crown or in the front, but there are certain tricks to effective curling without sending your tresses up in smoke. It takes some practice to get the hang of it, so try first with a cool iron--catching your hair in it, wrapping, and then winding it up--until you feel entirely comfortable with the twisting motion that is required. (It helps to comb flat the section of hair you want to curl before you clip it against the surface of the curling iron.) Once the iron is hot, you must work fast; **a curling iron requires only about thirty**

seconds per section of hair to work. The same principle applies to curling irons as to roller setting; the larger the section, the looser the curl. You may also use your hot rollers as a curling iron: simply let one get very hot (at least ten minutes on the rod) and then--holding it by its spikes--wrap your hair around it where you want to spot curl.

The trick here is *not* to clip it in, but to hold it for a minute as you would a curling iron, then gently unwind.

Obviously you need to be very careful using this kind of intense, direct heat on processed or damaged hair.

THE WET SET

*W*et setting is enjoying a resurgence in popularity these days since perms have become much more common. Perms allow you great styling flexibility...if you know how to set your hair. A perm can always be left to dry naturally, of course; it can also be the solid underpinning of an interesting set.

If you set, consider a *natural* set that is easy on the hair and gives you a lovely soft look.

NATURAL HAIRSETTING

*Y*ou probably already have what you need in your closet or medicine chest: cotton, to make rollers that will not pull or break the hair, and toothpicks, to hold them. To make a roller, break off cotton in two- to three-inch lengths (each will be about three-quarters of an inch thick) and roll and press into shape.

Here's how to get a new look with an old-fashioned set:

1

Wash your hair and allow it to dry partially.

2

Apply a setting lotion by combing through hair.

3

Wrap hair around cotton, then roll up and fasten by sticking a toothpick through the middle--and under--the roller, or use two clips at the sides. Make sure not to wrap hair too tight, or the roller will squash.

4

Let hair dry naturally...if you have the time. If not, use a hand-dryer.

5

After removing roller, **finger-comb into shape**.

PINCURLS

*E*verybody knows how to make pincurls, but I have a few suggestions:

1

Use clips, rather than bobby pins (which damage your hair and your teeth).

2

Make stand-up curls instead of those that are flattened to the scalp.

Hair should be slightly damp, but still wet enough to work with. Wrap a section around one finger and clip it to itself at the root. For a looser curl, use two or three fingers to make the loop and clip the same way.

If you are not afraid of an even more extreme look, you might try using those old-fashioned "wave clips" that were so popular in the forties.

PERMS AND BODYWAVES

Perms and bodywaves, which are just gentler perms, done on larger rollers so that there is buoyancy rather than curl-are a good way to maintain a look and give your styling more life with almost no time investment past the initial processing. Traditionally, if you had very little natural body (curl or wave) in your hair, you would get a permanent wave so your set would hold from week to week. (Can you *imagine*!) Now, however, this kind of chemical processing is much more likely to be done simply to give your hair a little lift and movement...and most women expect not to have to set at all once they have a perm or bodywave. In a way, permanent waving has gone from being an expression of everything about hairstyling that we reject today (stiff, set, styled "hats" of hair)...to the ultimate in convenience.

CAUTION: PERMING IS PROCESSING

The chemicals that make the wave or curl break down the structure of the hair so it can be reshaped around the curling rods. This process is then stopped by a neutralizer that "freezes" the hair strands into their new shape.

Perming is literally permanent, because while the curl *will* relax somewhat over time, the hair's structure itself is altered the only way to rid yourself of a perm is to grow it out or cut it off. This means you must carefully evaluate what you want from a perm and how you want it to look, as well as assess the shape your hair is in (your hairdresser can be your closest ally in this, whether s/he does the perm in the salon, or you do it at home yourself). There is no question that *your results with a perm are directly related to the condition of your hair before you get one*. If your hair is damaged already, you can either wait till it grows out, cut off the damage, or spot perm selectively to avoid reprocessing already processed hair.

A good perm should last four to six months. The hair can then be repermed, although I don't like doing so more than twice a year. You never know when the hair will just "give up" and emerge from its last perm looking like a helmet of feathers.

TIMING IS ALL

Whether you do your perm yourself or have it done in a salon, the most critical aspect of perming is keeping a careful watch on the chemical process.

Personally **I prefer the quicker cold wave** (which takes five to ten minutes); I think there is less room for error, since I can tell immediately what is happening on hair I can actually touch (*I constantly* check the "rate of wave"), and I'm less sure about what is going on across the room under a dryer for the half hour or so the heat perms require. Moreover, my experience with heat-activated perms is that they can "take" unevenly, perhaps because of the air patterns in a dryer or the way the person sits. I'd rather have as much control as is practical.

This is the kind of control you should strive for when you wave your hair at home. Check a curl every couple of minutes to make sure the processing action hasn't suddenly speeded up; what I look for to indicate "ready" is the appearance of a ridge in the hair when a rod is loosened. I always feel it is best and safest, by the way, to **choose the largest rod that will do the job**, and to **underperm slightly**.

CREATIVE PERMING

*T*here are lots of interesting things you can do with perming by varying the sizes of rods and the ways they are placed (long gone is the poodle look of the overall littlerod permanent wave). The first thing you want to do, however, is get your hair ready for the perm.

Plan to **have your hair cut before you get your perm**. This helps to remove damaged hair and split ends that can make a horror of even the best perm. Your hair should be clean and damp when you start.

You should also be clear in your own mind--and discuss this quite explicitly with whoever will be perming your hair if you're having it done at a salon--just *how much curl* you want. In the late sixties and early seventies, everybody was into a cloud of frizz standing away from the scalp...even if you started out with dead-straight hair. In the last decade, the trend has been toward softer and softer curl...sometimes so little that (like a great face-lift) it is almost impossible to tell anything has been done--you just look better. It is easy to get carried away and overperm, so if you want a bodywave (which means almost no visible curl), make that clear. And if you want loose curls rather than tight ones, make that clear, too.

SPOT PERMS

Sometimes the whole head does not need to be permed; for instance, you might just want some lift at the crown (you can do this for long hair as well as short), because this is often the area that goes flat first. And there are other times when damage (at the temples, say) dictates that you not process that particular patch of hair anymore.

You can also refresh a tired perm without redoing the whole head by spot perming. Perm just what you want and leave the rest to grow out a little longer (hair does not, as you well know, grow at the same rate all over the head).

Bodywaves are not just for people with limp, straight hair, however. Sometimes even people with fairly curly hair find that a bodywave tames curl and helps the hair to look more stylish.

STRAIGHTENING

Straightening is simply perming hair straight. It is the same process without the rollers.

I don't much care for straightening; I love the vitality and youthful look of *managed* curly hair. People with curly hair who get it straightened, it seems to me, end up with hair that looks a lot less natural and "bright," not only because curly hair tends to be more fragile and brittle, and so responds less well to chemical processing, but also because while it may be nearly impossible to tell whether someone has a perm or bodywave, you can almost always spot straightened hair. It's a little old-fashioned, like "set" hair.

If you feel you must straighten, you should go to a salon to have it done. And go to someone who has experience with your kind of hair and with the straightening process itself: if you overperm, you can often hide damage and problems with skillful cutting, but if you overstraighten, breakage will *show*. Spot straightening may be the better strategy, giving you the effect of less frizz by allowing just the hairline to forelock to blend in with the rest of the hair.

COLORING AND WAVING

When you plan both to color and wave your hair, you must be aware that you are intending a double insult to it, raising the chances of something going wrong so that--one way or the other--you end up overprocessed.

Perms should always be done before coloring, as they lighten the hair's color (natural or no) at least a shade…and they may lift artificial color in unpredictable ways. **The very *least* span of time between perming and coloring should be a week, and preferably two or three weeks.**

STYLING WITH GELS AND MOUSSES

*T*hese gloppy styling aids are the beauty industry's latest hot sellers. Unfortunately, not enough people really know how to use them, so they tend to collect in the back of the medicine chest along with all the other beauty stuff you have bought and found "didn't work."

Mousses and gels can be a lot of fun to use--if you know how--because they let you create effects that cannot be gotten any other way. I prefer them for spot styling, but some people don't mind using them as an all-purpose styling aid. One thing you are going to want to keep in mind when you use mousses and gels--as when you use anything on your hair is that they can be drying and damaging to delicate hair (many of them contain alcohol), as well as gummy on oily hair. They also leave a residue that can build up, even with daily washing, and they may make your scalp itch, flake, or burn.

These aids are especially interesting to use to produce sculptured effects that accentuate the good points of your face and play down poor ones--slicking back the sides, building height at the top, manipulating bangs so that they spike, or curl...or do whatever you want.

HOW TO USE GELS AND MOUSSES

*B*oth gels and mousses can be used as setting lotions, although they may leave you with very stiff hair. Once one of these compounds has dried, it can be a problem to comb hair or otherwise "break" a style, depending on what you have used (the European gels are the worst offenders), your hairstyle can collapse completely and leave a blizzard of tiny gel bits in your hair and on your clothes. (If you *don't* disturb it, though, gel will give you a slick, wet look.) Some of the mousses, on the other hand, can be combed out and function more like a super-setting lotion.

   If this is what you want to do, start with slightly damp hair, although your hairstyle should be well on its way to where it is going. If you are using mousse, you will need a palmful to style your hair; if you are using a gel, a glob the size of a dime should do it. Mousse can be massaged into hair and then the hair "scrunched" and pushed into a style. Gel is used much more like old-fashioned brilliantine: slick on, then comb or push your hair into place. In both cases, let the style set until the mousse or gel has dried. You'll have to experiment to see which products you can play with after they have dried and which leave you worse off than when you began.

   If you would like to make your own mousse, here is a recipe for one that sounds so delicious you may want to eat the leftovers!

Tasty Hair Mousse

2 egg whites	1 teaspoon rose or lavender fragrance
½ cup coconut oil	2 capsules vitamin E

Beat the egg whites until they form stiff peaks, then add other ingredients. Let set half an hour. Now apply sparingly and gently scrunch the ends.

HIGH-STYLE HAIR

*E*very once in a while I work with a client who wants something *really* different...even bizarre. This is a kick to do occasionally, but it certainly doesn't make up the major part of my work--even here in high-style New York City.

There are very few people--women or men--who either like, look good, or are in a position to wear some farout style. It is easier to get away with if you are young, very good-looking, or in the arts, but you're unlikely to see something too wild waltzing out of my salon.

I can (and do) high-style hair with the best of them. Also, because I really like people--and especially some of the women clients I work with--I like to see them looking *pretty*...and it's hard to look pretty with a Mohawk--even a modified Mohawk.

Think carefully about an especially trendy look. You may have to live with it a long time...as a shmohawk.

CHAPTER 9

Finishing Touches

Whether you go for the natural method of styling or prefer the help of some sort of a set, there are ways to finish off your styling that will give it the best of "the hairdresser look."

My way of finishing is to work the hair with my hands--pulling bits of it straight here, pushing a wave into it there, achieving height by literally lifting the hair away from the scalp. I love this sort of natural, tousled look because it has so much movement and individuality and because it is impossible to mess up. When you leave my chair and pull your sweater over your head, or step out into the street and get blown apart by the wind, or go home and sleep on it, you can't wreck this kind of look. It will always be a little different--depending on how you run your fingers through it or where the wind blows it--but the basic styling will not vanish with some particular hair-by-hair arrangement that needs to be glued in place.

You may be one of those people, however, who prefers a sleeker, smoother, more sophisticated look or who wants a special effect. There are smashing finishes for you, too.

BRUSH-SMOOTHING

This is the time to use that natural-bristle brush you used to pull at your hair with...and I hope I have weaned you from it for any purpose but styling. (See "Brushing" in Chapter 2 if you want to refresh your brush knowledge.)

Spray the styling brush with the very lightest mist of spritz, setting lotion, or hairspray--just enough to get those little frazzly things under control--and then pass it gently over the hair. **Don't spray the hair directly for finishing.**

This works well for styles that depend on a certain sleekness for their effect, whether they are curly, wavy, or relatively straight.

TEASING

Surprise: I'm no fan of teasing. Now and then, however, the very gentlest, most judicious bit of **back-combing can support a style** that needs special height or width. Unless your hair has a great deal of body, and you are fortunate enough to have it growing in just the right direction to lend the necessary support to your chosen style (some people do have this), you may need to back-comb--just a little!--to get the look you want.

HERE'S HOW TO BACK-COMB WITH THE LEAST AMOUNT OF DAMAGE:

- Use a comb that has fine teeth so you can get the job done with dispatch.
- Assess exactly where you need this little bit of help and then mentally divide up the portion of hair that will need to be done into patches about an inch long and half an inch wide. (Using more hair means you lose control over the backcombing and often have to do more than necessary to get the effect you want.)
- *Keep the comb near the roots* of the hair; you never want to get out toward the end--not only because what you are doing is not supposed to show, but because the ends are more delicate. You want the hair to fold back on itself halfway down its length. This will also give you a longer-lasting "tease."
- Little by little, back-comb that portion of hair you will use as a "cushion" for styling and then, before smoothing it over, use the fingers near the scalp to loosen the back-combing slightly. Push the cushion into place. (Don't be afraid to use your hands!)
- When you have pushed in the general shape you seek, use your finishing brush to smooth in the style. Take care that none of the superstructure shows through the covering hair.
- The final effect should be one of natural springiness, not of some armature under your hairdo. Your hair should still be able to move.

For the most natural teased look, finger-comb your hair into its basic shape after washing until it's almost dry, then back-comb while it is slightly damp. Alternate between spritzing and gentle back-combing until you achieve the look you want.

HOLDING A STYLE: SPRITZES AND GOOP

I believe in using substances on the hair that nourish, sleek, or protect it...or all three. As far as I know, this eliminates traditional hairsprays-- which only hold, and do that with an ingredient very like lacquer. Stay away from this stuff! It's death on the hair, and there are better ways to hold it...although who would want immobile hair?

SPRITZES

*T*hese are my favorite things to use to refresh curl, dampen for a set, or "lay over" the finished style for a little shine and control. Spritzes are *not* hairsprays; they are very diluted mixtures of water and some

other ingredient with the capacity to hold or sleek lightly when dry. A spritz should also add a little body and shine and should not contain any substance that can damage your hair: my Fleuremedy line has a spritz made of flower and herb extracts that add luster and help make hair more manageable; it is a sort of all-purpose refresher.

Many of the recipes I have already given you can be used as a spritz...if you simply apply it with a mister. (Part of what makes a spritz a spritz is the capacity of the applicator to spray a fine mist that will distribute itself evenly over your hair; bottles with mister tops into which you can put your preparations are widely available.)

The grapefruit/lemon "Hair Freshener" (Chapter 7) is just right for this. You can also use the beer/water setting lotion (Chapter 8) as a spritz. Or the herbal and floral waters (Chapter 3), or the "Herbal Treatment for Dry Hair" (Chapter 5), or even the "Gleam Rinse" (Chapter 3). Or try the blond or brunette tonics if your hair is not processed (Chapter 2).

I suggest keeping a couple of different spritzes around (in the fridge, so they stay fresh). Then you can use the one that suits your mood or your hair's needs on a given day. Try it--you'll like it! And you'll be rewarded with more manageable, healthier hair, and good feeling about what you're doing for it.

You might also consider carrying around a tiny mister in your bag (Fleuremedy Spritz, for instance, comes in a purse size) for during-the-day hair refreshing.

GOOP

My concept of "goop" includes not only the mousses and gels I have already mentioned, but the old-fashioned brilliantines and pomades that are still produced (in small quantity and great quality) in Europe. Pomades were in use long before mousse and gel were thought of, and they are undoubtedly the forerunners of these popular styling aids.

Today, gel/mousse and pomade are very different products: gel/mousse can be used to sculpt a style, while a pomade should be used to control, sleek, and add shine to one. They also have fundamentally different formulations. gel/mousse is water-based, so it feels soapy going on and dries hard (although the stiffness can be brushed out, leaving the set in), while pomade is oil-based. My own Fleuremedy Pomade has been devised with conditioning oils to help lessen potential damage to the hair.

SCRUNCHING WITH MOUSSE OR GEL

My favorite way of using these water-based products is not as a setting lotion, but as a finisher. If you want a relatively light finish, use a mousse; if you want something with a little more control and holding power, try a gel, which is really just a mousse without the air in it.

Scrunching is another hands-on technique, and you have to be one of those people who don't mind tossing the salad with your hands to use it regularly. What you will want to do is get the gel down near the roots of your hair, and then **give your style structure by taking fingerfuls of hair and squeezing and twisting--scrunching--at the scalp**. (To do this effectively, hair can't be too long; the look you want is fairly punky, so the scrunch--unlike regular teasing--should show and actually be part of the look.)

Clearly this is not for everyone, but it is a lot of fun for those who like the look.

POMADE

*P*omade can be terrific on curly or straight hair--wherever you aren't afraid of adding oil to the hair and scalp. (Don't say "no" to yourself too quickly; contrary to what you might think, this can help the look of

your hairstyle even if your hair *is* oily by making a virtue of the heavier, shiny look. It also protects the hair shaft itself.) You have to decide, however, whether this is the look you want, since there are some hairstyles that do not benefit at all from the sheen and weight added by a pomade--a blunt-cut style, for instance. But if your hair is curly and won't wilt (black hair can look especially wonderful with the glisten of pomade), or if you have straight hair that you either want to comb straight back or slick into a chignon, pomade can be a real discovery.

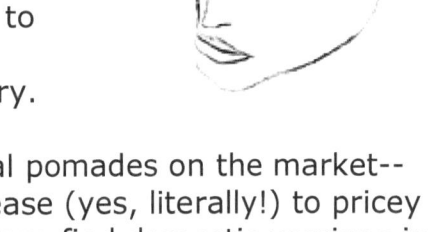

As I suggested, there are commercial pomades on the market--everything from old-fashioned bear grease (yes, literally!) to pricey European concoctions. You can sometimes find domestic versions in

147

beauty supply stores that have a black clientele...but just be sure you read the label carefully to check for substances that are potentially harmful to your hair.

If you want to make a down-home version of pomade, here is the recipe I use on my own hair:

Richard's Pomade

½ cup coconut oil
1 tablespoon jojoba oil
1 tablespoon apricot oil
2 capsules vitamin E
1 tablespoon favorite fragrance or flower of herb essence

Blend for 15 seconds. If mixture is too "wet," allow to chill in refrigerator. It will harden slightly. Keep in refrigerator.

Start off with about a teaspoonful of pomade, apply evenly through your hair. (You can always add more if you need it.)

CHAPTER 10

Color Me Carefully

THE GOOD NEWS ABOUT COLOR

Color used to be a sort of flat "mask" used by women who wanted to have more fun as a blonde or thought they were cheating age by covering gray. In short, it was seen as a kind of cure for self-image problems.

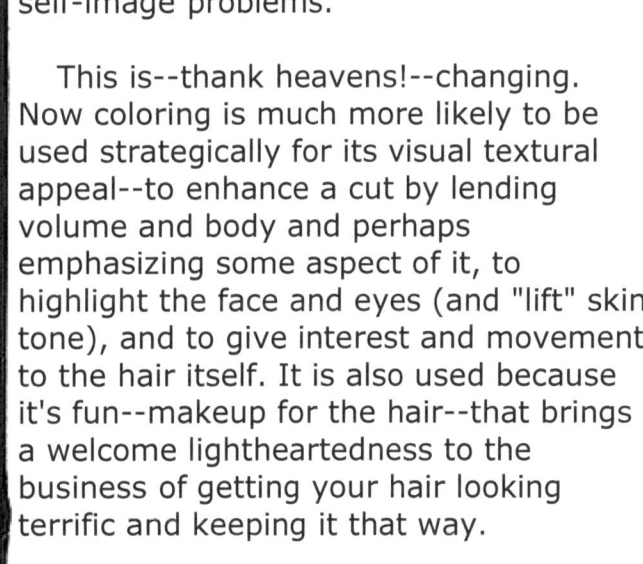

This is--thank heavens!--changing. Now coloring is much more likely to be used strategically for its visual textural appeal--to enhance a cut by lending volume and body and perhaps emphasizing some aspect of it, to highlight the face and eyes (and "lift" skin tone), and to give interest and movement to the hair itself. It is also used because it's fun--makeup for the hair--that brings a welcome lightheartedness to the business of getting your hair looking terrific and keeping it that way.

We have the new technologies to thank for this flexibility. All kinds of temporary color--cellophanes, rinses, hennas, hair mascara, spray-on color--have made hair coloring a more inviting adventure. Even one-step permanent coloring has supplanted the two-step process of stripping the hair and then coloring it.

MAKING THE DECISION

*W*hat people don't understand is that with today's technology a colorist is able to give you almost anything you want--pink, green, stripes...*anything*. As a client, therefore, you must be more thoughtful about the effect you want--and work closely with your colorist--so that within the nearly limitless range of possibilities you get exactly the effect you are looking for. Some of the new rinses (semipermanent color--see below for definitions) can be very useful for goof-proof experimentation that will come out after a couple of washings.

It is also important to consider the grow-out period before you take the plunge. Do you want to continue coloring, or are you looking for a "one shot" that will grow out gracefully? People who have colored their hair for years often continue to do so simply because they can't deal with the grow-out...or are afraid to find out how much gray they actually have. This seems a poor reason to go on doing something that can damage your hair.

We also have new techniques for doing the actual coloring; I think it would be fair to say it's much more an art than it ever was, with a great range of choice about what to do and how to do it. We can highlight, henna, warm, or brighten natural color. We can blend shades (sometimes as many as six) and layer--or grade--color for a much more natural look...or a special effect. We can cover just the gray or change the natural color completely. All this said, I still must reiterate that there is nothing more magnetic or enhancing than a beautifully cut and styled head of natural--yes, especially that gray/white/salt-and-pepper--hair that is clean, fresh-smelling, and lively.

A WORD ABOUT GRAY HAIR

I encourage people to show the gray. First of all, even if you do want to color it away, it is important to know just where it is, and most people color the whole head rather than just the hair that needs it. Not only does this spot approach make maintenance easier, but you avoid color buildup (which damages the hair and makes it look dull and gummy) because you are isolating the areas to be treated and lengthening the time between coloring. Also think in terms of lightening and brightening your own hair color instead of covering the gray; you can use semipermanent hair color without peroxide that makes the nongray hair very shiny and makes the gray "read" as highlights.

Never pull out your gray hair. You're not going to stop the natural signs of aging, but you are potentially damaging the hair follicles, and the older you get, the more you're going to need every hair you've got...whatever its color.

THE COLOR VOCABULARY

So many coloring terms are tossed around that sometimes it's hard to know what someone is suggesting. Here are some explanations that should help you decide what to do with your hair.

CELLOPHANES:

Cellophanes--or "jazzing," as it is sometimes called--is a new color technique in which the hair shaft is coated with what are sometimes pretty outlandish colors.

Cellophane colors can be "placed" and are therefore a good deal easier to control than all-over color. They stick well but don't lift natural hair color (this means no roots). Cellophanes don't work well on treated or very pale blond or gray hair, but they are a good way to get your feet wet with color.

GELS:

Gel colors are the lightweights: very temporary, hardly lasting from one shampoo to the next. They work well on white or gray hair and are especially suited to shorter styles that have a natural highlight, where the "laid over" color is more noticeable.

If you're interested in some of the less conventional colors, try aubergine, *real* red, or maybe even plum. *That* will turn heads!

HENNA:

Henna is a natural reddish vegetable dye that has been used at least since Egyptian times on the hair and body. The most primitive (and efficient) method of applying henna to hair was to make a thick paste of it and then apply it to the hair every hour during the heat of the day so the color was baked in. Nowadays, with the help of hairdryers, henna can be applied in forty-five minutes. The same paste is painted on the hair and covered with a plastic bag; then you sit under the dryer until you have just the right shade.

Nowadays, too, you can get henna in black and a honey-yellow color as well as the traditional red. Henna coats the hair shaft, so it can be protective, especially in the sun. It is also possible, however, to overhenna, so that the dye builds up, resulting in a Technicolor effect. Too much henna can cause terrible breakage; I have seen whole heads of hair broken off at the roots.

Henna lasts about eight weeks, depending on how often you wash your hair.

P.S. If you henna at home, *never* mix the henna preparation with any other synthetic dyes. You may end up with an unrecognizable mat of used-to-be-hair.

HIGHLIGHTING:

This has also been called streaking and frosting. The intention is to give a natural, sun-streaked effect by lightening and then using a series of different colors that will blend with the natural color.

Streaking used to be done in a rather barbaric fashion, using a plastic cap through which pieces of hair were pulled with a crochet hook. Not only did it hurt, but it often produced a striped effect. The foil method is more likely to be used now: very fine strands of hair are treated and wrapped in foil, which gives the colorist a good deal more control than the older method.

Hair painting is similar to highlighting. It's a technique in which smaller areas (usually just the front) are handpainted with color. Bleach isn't used.

HAIR MASCARA OR HAIR MAKEUP:

This is probably one of the safest ways to dress up the hair with fun colors. However, it works best on hair that is not heavily dyed or peroxided. It can stain somewhat, but generally it's effective for some hot streaks at night. Hair mascara works with all hair color types.

I endorse this kind of color most strongly, as it is probably the safest and most natural to use. Just make sure to treat the hair with conditioner after use.

PERMANENT AND SEMIPERMANENT COLOR

The fundamental difference between a permanent and semipermanent color (or rinse) is that **permanent color** contains peroxide and ammonia, so it **changes the structure of the hair** (by removing its outer coating) to prepare it to take the final color. Permanent color will give 100 percent coverage to graying hair and can be used to lighten hair, too (which cannot be done with any but permanent color).

Semipermanent color (rinse) coats rather than penetrates the hair shaft, but because it does not lighten hair, it doesn't fade like peroxide color. It is, however, a bit more permanent than is usually represented, lasting about two months; so be careful.

Rinses are easy on the hair and great to use for all kinds of relatively temporary needs: trying out a new color (I almost always recommend them over permanent color for a first-timer); covering gray (they will cover about 20 percent of gray hair); or doing an interim coloring job while a problem grows out.

TAKING THE PLUNGE

So you want a change. What are your options? Blonds almost always want to go lighter and brighter. Brunettes may *think* they want lighter hair or streaks; what they usually need is warmer highlights--ambers, russets, or even a tortoiseshell blend of lighter and darker. Women with gray hair most often simply want it gone...and may do much more than is necessary to get rid of it. (You presumably want to get rid of the *problem*, not necessarily change your hair color entirely.)

In each case the issue is not only what color to use and how much of it, but the placement of that color for maximum effect and least overall processing. The trend now is to keep color somewhat away from the scalp (I feel that this "double-tone" effect gives a depth to the hair) and to vary it, either in shade or intensity or placement.

Do be aware that **coloring will change the feel of your hair**. The nice way of describing this alteration is that it gives more volume and body; the less appealing way is to say that the hair feels "heavy." Permanent hair coloring actually swells the hair shaft as it penetrates (except with the lightest and darkest colors, which tend to make the hair limp), literally making the hair thicker. You may find, therefore, that coloring your hair will make it more manageable. The trick here is to avoid color buildup: less is more.

WHAT COLOR? AND HOW MUCH OF IT?

*I*t's virtually impossible to comment on **complete color changes**, except to note that they are **hard on your hair, hard to achieve** (with any semblance of naturalness), **and hard to keep up**. Much more practical and versatile are the subtler kinds of coloring that enhance your hair's (and your skin's) natural color.

Following are suggestions and recipes for color enhancements (and recommendations for dealing with gray) for every shade of hair--both at home and in the salon. If you are color treating, by the way, keeping your hair shiny is difficult. That's why I'm beginning with an all-purpose hair gentler for color-treated hair that you can use in conjunction with the rest of the remedies (where directed). It will leave your hair wonderfully clean and shiny even after a couple of shampoos.

Molasses Treatment for Color Enhancement

Shampoo and towel-dry hair. Mix 2 tablespoons of blackstrap molasses with 1 tablespoon conditioner. (For longer hair, double the recipe.) Apply to hair and blend through from roots to ends.

Leave on 20 minutes (try relaxing in the bathtub) and rinse thoroughly.

COLOR ENHANCING

LIGHT BLOND HAIR

- AT HOME: To brighten hair, mix ordinary (2 percent) hydrogen peroxide with lemon juice in a spray bottle. Spray into hair and rinse. This gives body and shine with little actual color change.
- AT THE SALON: Because your own coloring is likely to be very fair, your colorist should *highlight* your hair in very pale blond. This must be done carefully because your hair is likely to be fragile. If your hair is also thin or fine, avoid any kind of all-over color, which will only make it seem thinner and finer.
- FOR GRAY: Highlighting in pale blond is the best way to deal with this shade of graying hair.

BLOND HAIR

- AT HOME: Same as light blond hair, but add the molasses treatment. Don't worry about the color of the molasses; it rinses out completely.
- AT THE SALON: The best method for virtually maintenance-free hair color is to highlight, especially by picking up (or picking out) the "line" of your styling.
- FOR GRAY: Because I am so partial to warm enhancements (especially for aging hair and skin), I like to see honey tones added to blond-gray hair, rather than those silvery-looking frosts.

LIGHT BROWN HAIR

- AT HOME: Mix the molasses treatment with three tablespoons of *strong* chamomile tea. Saturate hair, then leave mixture on for one hour with a plastic bag over it (to retain heat and moisture).

    You'll end up with gentle blond highlights...and lots of shine and body.

- AT THE SALON: Light brown hair is the chameleon of the hair family: you can do almost anything with it colorwise. You may want ashy highlights or a warmer, Titian color--either all over or just highlighting the face. Think creatively about "sprays" of color--especially at the ends of the hair. Or, if your hair is healthy, you may want to go all out with one of the newer tortoiseshell or layered colors.
- FOR GRAY: Consider a semipermanent rinse... not to cover the gray, but to blend it in and make it look like highlighting. For gray, always use warm tones that are a few shades lighter than your own.

MEDIUM-BROWN HAIR

- AT HOME: Consider applying henna to your hair; you can buy home henna kits wherever you get personal care and beauty items.

    Henna can be tricky on lighter hair because as a vegetable dye it has an unpredictable uptake and can color unevenly. With darker hair, however, this isn't a problem. Henna will give your hair body, sheen, and wonderful russet highlights...and it's *good* for it.

    Henna treatments should last about eight weeks, depending on how often you wash your hair.

- AT THE SALON: With your darker hair, you have lots more room to play around with color. You may even want to try one of the more daring color rinses or cellophane colors, like raspberry, aubergine, or sunflower yellow. These colors lie over your own, look perfectly smashing when, the light hits a certain way, and are nearly invisible at other times. If you want to have some fun, yours is the ideal hair color for it.
- FOR GRAY: If you have 10-20 percent gray, use a non-hydrogen peroxide rinse that is a couple of shades lighter than your own (nongray) hair. This formula will not change the color of the brown (although it will brighten it), but it will turn the gray hair into soft highlights.

If you have 25-50 percent gray, and are determined to be rid of it, you need a detailed consultation with your colorist. Permanent color will be required, and this means more color maintenance at the salon and considerably more care and vigilance on your part: you should use a nonstripping shampoo and always condition, and you need to remember that both sun and chlorine will have a damaging effect on hair *color* as well as the hair itself.

DARK BROWN/BLACK HAIR

- AT HOME: Henna is the best thing for you to use. Try the red shades for auburn highlights, blond shades for body and shine.
- AT THE SALON: Experiment as above or go for red highlights (*not* blond—they turn coppery in a very unappealing way). Highlighting is still a good way to give the *illusion* that all your hair is lighter without having to strip it down and recolor it.
- FOR GRAY: Resist the temptation to resort to permanent all-over color; nature knows best when she fades our hair with the rest of

us as we age, and there is nothing older or harder--or more artificial looking--than dark-dyed hair.

Stick with a couple of shades lighter than your natural color for a rinse to make the gray look like lighter streaks. And if you have so much gray that you are considering a complete color change, speak to your colorist. S/he needs to know not only about your hair, but about your life-style: How often do you shampoo? Are you active in sports so that your hair is exposed to water and sunlight? How do you intend to wear it? The safest choice in these cases is a warm color, which tends to last longer and look better when it is "insulted."

CARING FOR COLOR-TREATED HAIR

Once again, *even if you are using something other than permanent color, these are chemicals, and chemicals can cause trouble*. There is always at least a *little* damage when you color your hair, and you need to think about this when you take care of that hair as well as when you get the color redone.

Color--even permanent color--will fade just from washing; if you get out into the sun, you will see changes from oxidation much more quickly (your hair may lighten up to two whole shades--which is never a good idea unless you have one of the few reds that actually improve in the sun). Ordinarily, you want to **avoid coloring more than once every six months**... and it can take a year for real damage to grow out.

It is, of course, much easier to keep tabs on the condition of your hair--and to control the recoloring schedule--if you don't succumb to coloring your whole head. Rely instead on spot coloring to keep your hair looking good, and you will be rewarded with more natural-looking hair as well as painless grow-out. (People seem much less worried about roots showing these days, perhaps because we have grown used to the multicolored effects.)

Here is a special conditioner you may want for your hair if you use color:

Rum Conditioner

2 egg yolks   1 tablespoon rum

Beat egg yolks until lemon-colored, then add rum and beat again. Massage through hair and wrap in towel. Leave on for half an hour while relaxing in the tub, then shampoo and rinse thoroughly with cool water.

PART

4

SEASONAL HAIR

I like to think that any given hairstyle has its seasons and can and should be adapted to changing weather and mood. (Hair also has its special care needs *in* each season--whether it is subjected to sun or the biting wind, to the stickiness of high humidity or the crackle of winter dryness.)

Changing your hair from season to season may be done through cutting, altering the texture (the body or curl), lifting or subduing the color slightly, or dressing it in a special way.

A nod to the change of seasons can also be made through the things you use on your hair to clean, condition, and nourish it...especially where scent--a sort of portable aromatherapy-is concerned: who doesn't have vivid memories of hair that smells delicately floral and fresh on the first days of spring? Of summer hair that recalls the sweet heat and cool aroma of an herb garden? Or the warmth and muskiness of hair on the first cold days? Or the excitement and tingle of spice on hair in the winter cold? Why not extend the pleasure in your crowning glory to all your senses?

Recipes in this chapter, therefore, are especially important for their "aromatherapeutic" value.

Summer

I am going to begin with summer because I think this season is hardest on hair...or rather, we *allow* things to happen to our hair in summer that are especially hard on it. We subject it to salt water and chlorine (which can turn color-treated hair green); we sit in the sun and burn it (hair burns just the way your skin does); and because too many of us love that sun-streaked look, we insult our hair further by putting harsh stuff on it to strip it and make it blonder...and then sit in the sun *again* to damage and fade it even more.

When I think of summer, I think protect, protect, protect. Skin, scalp, hair: all need special protection from the ravages of the outdoor life. And what is past protection needs special *attention*.

PROTECTING YOUR HAIR

*T*he best all-around protection for your hair (as well as your skin) is to shade it by wearing a hat or staying out of the sun altogether.

This is unrealistic for most of us, however, with our very active lives, so the next best solution is to **coat the hair strands--and protect the scalp--with** some substance that will give your hair a fighting chance. And the best substance I know of is **a mixture of a good sunscreen and a cream rinse or conditioner**. Mix, work into your hair, and then comb through with a wide-toothed comb for even distribution. Slick back your hair. (Who likes hair hanging in her face in the sun?) This looks sleek, pretty, and summery and gives your hair a sort of hot-pak as you sun. Don't forget to reapply every hour or so to refresh the mixture's effectiveness, and be sure to give yourself a generous reanointment after a swim.

When you wash your hair after sunning, don't use any more conditioner. What remains in your hair will be quite enough to take care of your conditioning needs.

HOMEMADE PRE-SUN CONDITIONERS

*I*f you like the idea of making your own conditioner and don't feel you need that extra sunscreen protection, here are two slickers that you can make for sunning and swimming. Wash them both out thoroughly *after* sunning.

Pre-Sun Conditioner for Dry Hair

1 tablespoon ground or crushed sage

1/2 cup avocado oil

1/2 cup coconut oil, warmed

Contents of 3 vitamin capsules

1 tablespoon favorite fragrance

Mix well. Rub through hair and then comb back smooth and sleek.

Pre-Sun Conditioner for Oily Hair

1 1/2 cups seaweed (gather it yourself!) or kelp

1 tablespoon sage

1 tablespoon crushed nettles

1 tablespoon rosemary oil

Process in blender until seaweed is pureed with other ingredients. Apply as above.

COLOR LIFTS FOR SUMMER

*T*he easiest lift for that streaked effect people like so much is very old-fashioned, and if your hair is not fragile--better yet, if it is a little oily--you can use a lemon juice rinse to tone your scalp, get rid of excess oil, and restore natural highlights to *naturally* blond or light-brown hair (this is not a good idea if your hair has been permed or color-treated):

Lemon juice Highlight Restorer

> Mix juice of 1 lemon with 1 cup water. Spritz
> or comb through hair. Let dry in the sun.

For some people, this kind of natural lightener works wonderfully well; the result is hair that looks like it belongs to kids who live outdoors. The older one gets, however, and the more one's hair has been through, the less likely it is that this method will be successful: your hair can end up looking faded and haystack-y instead of becomingly streaked. And please, please, **don't use peroxide**--*in the sun or out*. You will get brassy orange instead of blond.

To counteract the fading effects of the sun and play up the highlights and color your hair already has as well as its shine, try these natural rinse/conditioners:

Summer Rinse for Blonds

1 tablespoon distilled white vinegar

1 cup water

Juice of 1/2 lemon (strained)

Mix ingredients well and pour through hair after shampooing, massaging, and working with fingers. Rinse gently with clear water.

Summer Rinse for Redheads

3 ounces fresh (or frozen) raspberries

1 teaspoon red wine vinegar

3 ounces fresh (or frozen) strawberries

Blend for 20 seconds and then comb through hair after shampooing. Let set for a couple of minutes and then rinse out.

Summer Rinse for Light-Brown Hair

1/2 cup plain yogurt

1/2 cup blackstrap molasses

1/2 cup coffee grounds

Stir ingredients together in a small bowl and massage into clean hair. Comb through to distribute.

Leave on for 20 minutes and then rinse well.

Summer Rinse for Chestnut or Blue-Black Hair

3 ounces fresh (or frozen blueberries)

2 tablespoons Fleuremedy (or other) Conditioner

1/2 cup blackstrap molasses

Stir together until well blended. Comb through hair after shampooing and leave on for 20 minutes. Rinse well.

SUMMER HENNA TREATMENTS

Another way to protect hair that is not color-treated from sun, salt water, and wind, while intensifying color and adding vibrancy and sparkle, **is to use henna**, which is a natural vegetable compound that protects the hair shaft while adding depth to its color. Henna won't give you the brassiness that too often follows overexposure of processed hair.

Some think only people with red highlights in their hair can use henna. With the new henna compounds this is not true: as discussed previously, blonds will see their hair lifted half a shade, while women with darker hair will find it gives their natural color a richness and warmth. Most everyone who uses henna is rewarded with added body and sheen.

Henna for Natural Blond Hair

2 cups natural henna (I like Collura's Wheat Blonde Shade)

1 tablespoon coconut oil

1/2 cup water

1/2 cup loose chamomile tea leaves (unbleached)

1/2 cup marigold petals

1/4 cup lemon juice (strained)

Henna for Natural Brunette Hair

2 cups henna (natural)

1 tablespoon rosemary oil

1 cup extra-strong black coffee

1/2 cup rosemary

Blend ingredients until mixture forms a thin paste (you may add a little extra lemon juice or coffee if it seems too thick).

Apply henna mixture at the roots of hair and comb through until hair is completely covered.

Swathe the head in a plastic bag, as airtight as possible.

Warm under a heat cap or dryer set medium hot or sit in the sun!--for 45 minutes. Wash out with *three separate applications* of diluted shampoo and then rinse thoroughly.

REPAIRING SUN DAMAGE

*E*ven the best-laid plans for hair protection can go awry...just as the occasional sunburn is probably inevitable. If you've had too much sun, here is a wonderfully soothing remedy for sunburned hair and scalp:

Sunburn Soother

1 cup plain yogurt
1/2 cucumber
1 avocado
1 egg
1 tablespoon wheat germ oil

Process in blender. Rub mixture through wet hair and massage in gently.

Leave on under a shower cap for half an hour, then shampoo with cool water and rinse with herbal or floral rinse.

To restore lost shine to sunburned hair, use "Gleam Rinse." Here's the recipe again:

Gleam Rinse

Mix 1 part apple cider vinegar with 7 parts softened water. Use as an after-shampoo rinse and then gently towel-dry.

SUMMER HAIR STYLING

Summer is a great time to have fun with all those casual styles you wouldn't think of wearing during the rest of the year, except perhaps for active sport: braids and twists, corn rows, ponytails. The wonderful thing about these summer variations is that they can be adapted to all but the shortest hair. When you learn how to handle your hair, you can do almost anything with these "unmessers," even try combinations of them (braids and ponytails, for instance).

You can also make these very practical styles work for you for evening or for daytime sophistication, with variations on the chignon. Another possibility is to use combinations of braiding and twisting to achieve a very sophisticated look (if you keep your hair up and back and relatively severe).

BRAIDING

Braiding (or plaiting, as we say in England) is a style that is as old as civilization. It is obviously easier to braid longer hair, but short hair can be partly corn-rowed and partly braided to achieve what amounts to a braided effect.

Basically, braiding is the weaving of strands of hair together in a pattern. Hair can be flat-braided (the three-strand braid) or round-braided (the lanyard braid of four strands, which is harder to do but worth the effort because its 3-D effect is sounusual).

You can braid your hair "loose" from the head or attached to it (essentially corn rowing), and you can braid your three-strand braid (the one you are probably familiar with) inside out for another interesting effect. You needn't limit yourself to the traditional single braid down the back or to the two braids behind the ear, either: make as many braids as you like, and then wrap them around your head (a *very* pretty fairy-tale or medieval look) or braid the *braids* together.

You can also achieve a wonderful look by braiding your hair when it is damp (or just leave the braids you already have in place after swimming) and then letting it dry completely in the braid. When your hair has dried, either undo the bottoms of the braid and let your hair unravel naturally, or unbraid it completely and luxuriate in the Pre-Raphaelite, romantic look the ripples will give you.

HOW TO BRAID PROPERLY

*H*air that is damp and has at least *some* wave is easiest to braid; it curves better into the twists and weaves you are making. (People with straight hair often realize that if their hair is not damp when braided-and even sometimes when it is--little "sticks" and spikes of hair are forever popping out and make the braid look porcupine-y.)

Gels or mousses can help with this smoothing if your hair tends to stick out of a braid. Just comb the gel or mousse through your damp hair (don't use too much--allow it to be diluted by the wetness of your hair) and then braid before it dries, smoothing those little stray pieces back in carefully.

Once you've finished, hold the braid in with *covered* elastics (you can find these in the dime store). The little ones are best for all but the thickest hair because you need to do less winding. Try to avoid regular bare rubber bands, as they catch in your hair and are likely to tear it. If you don't like the look of the elastic holder, either cover it with a strand of hair from the braid itself or wrap a short length of ribbon around it. (One or more pieces of narrow ribbon can also be braided *through* the hair; this is lovely and quite festive!)

As pretty and convenient as braids are, people are sometimes not as careful as they might be to protect their braided hair. Remember:

1

Don't pull the braid too tight at the scalp; it can result in hair loss.

2

Avoid leaving the braids in too long: it can lead to breakage where the same area is consistently exposed.

CORN ROWING

Corn rowing is really a flat braid that is kept close to the head by picking up more hair along the scalp with each twist until the whole diameter of the head has been braided; then, if the hair is long enough, the braid can be continued into a regular free braid, although it will be anywhere from a little to a lot smaller than what one ordinarily thinks of as a braid.

While most corn rowing--especially that done with black/Afro hair, where corn rowing originated--is done with very few strands at a time (there may be literally hundreds of attached braids that may or may not swing clear of the head, depending on how long the hair is), corn rowing can also be done with more strands of hair at a time so there are relatively few braids--perhaps only a couple (one over each ear, for instance) with the rest of the hair left unbraided.

It is usually easiest to get someone else to corn row your hair for you: elaborate corn rowing is both exacting and laborious. The good news is that a skillfully done job--especially if your hair has enough natural curl to hold the braids--can last for weeks at a time; just wash your hair with the braids in.

Corn rows can also be dressed up with all kinds of decorations that are slipped right onto the braid from its loose end, so that the ornaments are held tight by the braiding itself. This is great fun and *sounds* wonderful (all that clicking and jingling!) in the summer.

CHIGNONS AND BUNS

Chignons (and buns, which are a sort of homelier version of chignons) have also been around for a very long time; they are traditionally worn by older and/or more sophisticated "ladies." Recent variations on the chignon, however (like the "washer-woman" style so popular about five years ago), show how the chignon/bun/twist can be adapted to anyone's hair and life-style.

    Basically the chignon effect is achieved by twisting and rolling the hair, then pinning it tight. One of the tricks to understanding how this works is to realize that if you take a hank of your hair and begin to twist, it will form *itself* into a bun or the more classic chignon form, a figure eight.

    This style is hard to fake with shorter hair, so you need to have enough length to twist the hair and have it coil itself into at least one tight circle. The knot then is held either with hairpins or one of the newer one-stick fasteners. There is even a version of the chignon that is pinless--who wants metal sticking into her head in the hot summer?

One variation that can be achieved with slightly shorter hair is what you probably know as the French twist, which is really more a method for fastening hair at the back of the head for a neat, small look. For this style, your hair only needs to be long enough to get it back (and gel or mousse can help in this); a row of hairpins holds the overlap that gives the impression of longer hair.

    All of these twist-and-knot alternatives are perfect for summer...and any other season when you want your hair to be sleek, sophisticated, and off your face. The beauty of chignons, twists, and buns for summer is that they needn't be so literally "up tight" (try pulling some hair around the face out of the knot, letting it fall so that it frames the features: a terrific, more casual look!), and they are wonderful for anybody with longer hair because their shapes and volumes are so versatile.

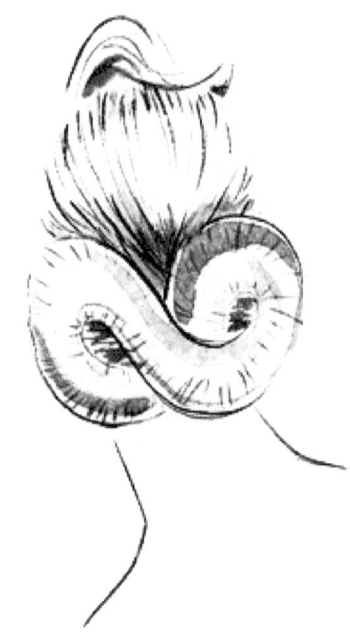

SPECIAL EFFECTS

*T*here are no two ways about it: I love flowers and herbs, and I use them however and whenever I can in and on hair.

Summer is absolutely the best time to take advantage of nature's bounty...and if you don't have your own garden to grow flowers and herbs for steeping (to make floral and herbal waters and other hair remedies), the produce stand and flower market are almost as good.

A dressed-up hairstyle on a summer evening looks even more dressed up with flowers. Stick one into a twist (perhaps a marigold as a spirit lifter), braid them right into your hair (daisies are hardy enough for this and will hold almost as long as your braid), or line the whole edge of a chignon with a series of tiny brilliant flowers like pansies. Tuck one behind your ear (one of those big, tropical looking beauties!) and think thoughts of exotic gardens and perfumed nights. Or--my favorite--make a classical garland (sew the flowers together with a large needle and dental floss, or use florist's wire for a less floppy version) and perch it on your shining glory.

Flowers can also be slipped under combs or over barrettes, and they're delicious combined with ribbons--especially the thin satin kind.

Don't limit yourself just to flowers, either. For centuries herbs have been used as talismans and restoratives...and they provide some of that wonderful aromatherapy I am always going on about. Parsley (for cleansing and allure) is the all-green version of baby's breath; or use basil leaves and sprigs of dill together for aroma and good luck. Chamomile will play up the highlights in your hair, and, as Shakespeare had Ophelia say, "There's rosemary, that's for remembrance...."

In short, *anything* natural tucked into your tresses will look pretty, smell nice, and bring you pleasure.

Fall

Fall seems to be the time to focus on repairing the damage we did during those last long dog days of summer when we were packing in every last ray of sun for the cold days to come. Let the first brisk day hit, and we are usually ready to leave summer behind and concentrate on pulling ourselves together again-getting organized, reassessing wardrobe and hair, being more *serious*...until next summer.

Take a careful look at the condition of your hair and scalp when you know you are finished summering. Now is the time to make your treatment/repair decisions...perhaps with the help of a professional.

DANDRUFF AND DRY SCALP

One of the most common after-summer problems is what appears to be dandruff but is in fact most often just a case of oversummered scalp.

Any of the moisturizers mentioned in Chapter 5 ("Keeping Hair Shiny")can be used to restore bounce and sheen to your hair and health to your scalp, but I have a particular favorite for the fall--"Apple-Mash Conditioner." It cleans the scalp of dead cells and nourishes your poor abused hair.

Apple-Mash Conditioner

2 apples, cut in pieces
½ cup plain yogurt
2 tablespoons apple cider vinegar

Put ingredients in blender and blend until smooth. Pour as much as needed through hair before washing and massage into scalp. Leave on for 10 minutes and then wash 3 times.

FALL COLORS

Autumn is the ideal time to rethink hair coloring...or perhaps to consider it if you haven't done it before. Both skin and hair can appear faded, and the kind of summer lightening that looked bright in the sun can look brassy indoors, especially when you get the sallow look that comes from a faded tan.

In my salon, we especially like warm tones for the hair in the fall. It seems just right for the mood of the season, and russets and tawny shades can bring a glow to any hair or complexion, although they work best on brown hair. This is another good time to consider using henna on your hair (which also reproteinizes).

We also have developed a special coloring process: protein gels. These are nonperoxide, nonammonia colors mixed with gelatin--perfect for highlights. To give that little extra life, we often blend these colors with real fruit blueberries, strawberries, and raspberries for dark hair; avocado, mango, and papaya for lighter hair.

TIME FOR A CHANGE?

You will probably need a good trim after the summer, and it is often in considering this fall cut that women decide on a more drastic alteration in style. You may also have gained or lost weight during the summer or changed your "look" in some way that is going to have an impact on what you decide to do about your hair. Many women start thinking of a slightly more finished look; fall is the time (perhaps because of old associations with the beginning of another school year) when you feel just a little bit more grown up. It is also the time when you are hefting those enormous fall issues of fashion magazines and thinking about wardrobe adjustments. If you haven't had a consultation recently with your hairdresser, now is the time: it is just the lift you need for facing the winter.

Winter

The major difficulties for hair in the winter are the heat and dryness (and static electricity) that are an inevitable part of the indoor environment. That's the bad news. The good news is the holidays; they brighten everyone up and give you more opportunities to dress up--and the license to do special things with your hair--than any other time of year. Let's deal with the problems first.

HAIR ELECTRIC

*J*ust as in the summer, you must be especially vigilant in the winter about hair damage, but this time the danger is not overexposure to the great outdoors but to the great *indoors*. Hair gets flyaway and dry. You brush it to make it shiny, and the ends split. The scalp dries out and itches (wool caps worn for warmth and the cycle of hot and cold don't help the condition of the scalp, either). And lots of us--especially people like me, who have curly hair--end up looking as if we've put our fingers in an electric socket.

Pay close attention during the winter months to your schedule for nourishing and conditioning hair and scalp: your usual program for maintaining shiny hair will need to be stepped up. Hot-paks are especially important in the winter, too, because they hydrate hair and scalp with deep moisturizing (see the hot-pak recipe in Chapter 5). And a spritz is the best antistatic remedy--one you can use throughout the day.

If you ski, give yourself a hot-oil treatment right under your hat. It works all day while you have fun (the secret is in the heating effect of the eucalyptus oil).

Ski-Pak

1 tablespoon eucalyptus oil

1 tablespoon rosemary oil

Mix together, rub well into hair, slick or tie back. Wrap hair in a scarf and then put on a ski hat. Leave oils on all day.

Later, shampoo well and rinse with "Gleam Rinse" or 1 part apple cider vinegar to 7 parts cool water.

When you get an attack of that itchy, static-y feel, try this hair freshener. It will revive hair and scalp in cold weather.

Après-Ski Hair Freshener for Static Electricity

Juice of half a lemon (strained)	1 pint Perrier or Evian water
Juice of half a grapefruit (strained)	

Mix together in a spray bottle or mister and use whenever hair threatens to get flyaway.

HOLIDAY HAIR

*H*olidays are your time to shine...and to let your creativity and fancy free. Even the simplest style can be transformed: this is when you can play with glitter in your hair or temporary color; pinecones, bells, and shiny little Christmas ornaments; garlands of tinsel or winter greens. If you never appear with curls, try *cascades* of them. And if you are truly adventurous, mousse your hair into fantastic shapes and decorate it with whatever you want. *Everything* is permissible during this festive time of year.

Spring

The weather is getting warmer. The air smells different. You feel as if you're coming alive again. It's spring.

What you really want to do is wake up your hair and scalp. And I can't think of a better way to do it than with the flowers and herbs that I love.

Spring Sauna Herbal Cap-Pak

Cut a double thickness circle of cheesecloth that will be large enough to fit your head (like a shower cap) when gathered at the edges with a string.

Between the thicknesses of this circle of cheesecloth, sprinkle and spread any combination of

Rose petals
Rosemary (brunettes)
Parsley
Chamomile (blonds)
Peppermint
Birch leaves
Crumbled cinnamon sticks
Sage

Sew around the edges of the circle with a large needle and string so that the herbs/flowers will be contained. Pull the string together at the edges and tie the cap firmly onto your head with all of your hair tucked up into it. Pour hot water over your head before you enter sauna or steam room (if you have access to them) or bath (if you don't). The fragrance will help you relax, and your hair will be conditioned and sparkling clean.

SPRING STYLING

When thoughts turn to spring cleaning and getting outside in the balmy air, it's probably time to ask yourself once again about the style you've been living with all winter. I'll bet you'd welcome a new feeling of being freed up and breezier.

A perm can be fun in the spring. Your hair may be limp after a long winter of dryness and being stuck under hats. In addition, many women cut their hair less regularly during the cold months and really need an invigorating trim, whether they want the extra boost of a perm or bodywave or not. Consider a styling that is a little more adventuresome; it will lift your spirits.

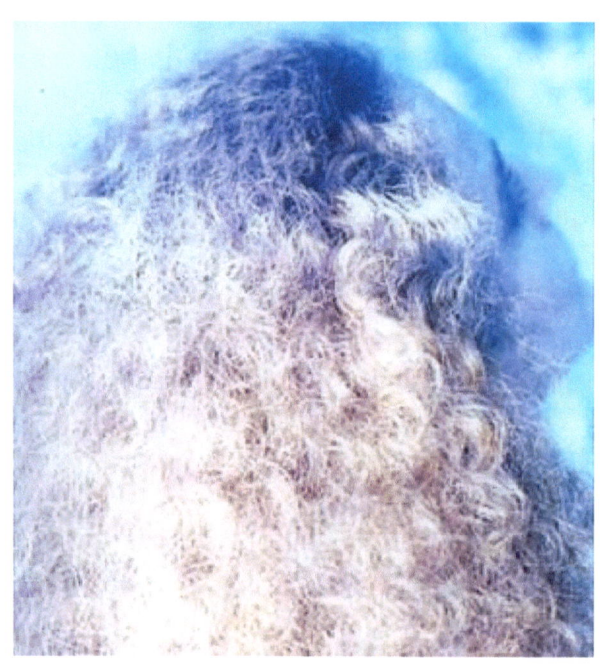

AFTERWORD

Celebrating Your Hair

So we've come full circle. And you have, I hope, been disabused of most of the anxiety-provoking myths about hair and haircare--and turned on by the potential of your *own* hair. In short, set free. Set free to live with your hair happily, to love it, to celebrate it.

Because nothing seems quite so real and relevant as actual examples, I chose six women to work closely with for the last section of this book. Each represents a different hair challenge, and each has life-style needs that require versatility and ease of handling throughout the day. Working with them gave me the opportunity to demonstrate how simple it is to achieve a variety of looks--one after another--with an excellent basic cut and a little imagination and flair. I want to stress that *anyone* can manage these changes. *Anyone* can have hair that she loves... every minute of the day and into the evening.

Everyone can be set free.

Sharon studies fine arts at the Parsons School of Design. At twenty, she is a wonderful combination of flair, style, and incandescent energy. Her day is nonstop and generally begins with a brisk early-morning walk.

Before hitting her stride along the pathways of Central Park, Sharon showered, washed, and conditioned her long hair, finger-dried it, then finished it with a blower and a large round brush to loosen and relax its extraordinary curl.

A long day of classes behind her, Sharon hurried back to her Columbus Avenue studio apartment for a quick metamorphosis from student of the arts to their appreciator--and she was off to a gallery opening on Madison Avenue, where her friend Michael's work was being shown. To reclaim a little of the sexy, untamed look of the morning, she spritzed her hair, then finger-combed it (with her head upside down) and scrunched the ends. This helped her feel refreshed as she also slipped in a little scalp massage.

It was Saturday night in Gotham, and Sharon had a major date with the major (currently, that is) man in her life--an evening of trendy dining and latenight dancing at The Tunnel. Such a special night cried out for special effects: flowers were tucked into the respritzed and revitalized curls, and pomade, deftly applied, helped to hold her hair, which she elegantly drew up and back off her neck.

Susannah is the youngest partner in a distinguished Wall Street law firm. A specialist in entertainment law, Susannah has a day that doesn't quit. Beginning at seven-thirty A.M., she moves at a hectic pace, inside the office and out, from meeting to meeting, from business lunch to drinks to client dinners, often running until the small hours.

Susannah needs wash-and-wear hair at its simplest. This morning she did nothing more than shampoo it and let it dry on its own, hand-shaping it because she was on the move.

And into her Gucci briefcase along with her contracts, letters of intent, and other weighty documents, she shrewdly tucked a canister of mousse for changes on the go.

For drinks at the Stanhope with a West Coast agent, Susannah smooths her hair to create a more sophisticated look (it depends on mousse for its sleekness).

Off to dinner in Soho with one of her most handsome movie star clients, Susannah merely spritzed her hair to reactivate the mousse, added a little more to ensure hold, and set her hair in large rollers in a random pattern. Mousse dries very quickly, so less than half an hour later she fingercombed her hair and teased it lightly (just at the roots) for a more dramatic effect. And for a final touch of glitz, she painted a few wild streaks of color with the new state-of-the-art hair mascara to match her dress.

Gabrielle is a socialite mover and shaker. Married to a real estate tycoon, she is the mistress of several households, including a country place in Bucks County and a Park Avenue triplex. She is also the mother of three. Between school board meetings, charity work, and black tie galas, Gabrielle barely has enough time to keep up with her macrocosmic marathon.

Relaxing after an invigorating seven-thirty A.M. session with Adah, her favorite exercise mistress, Gabrielle indulged herself in a mini-spa treatment in her own luxurious mirrored, marbled, and meticulously outfitted bath. Afterward, she simply air-dried her hair, lifting it away from the scalp periodically to encourage drying and the expression of its natural wave and body.

For an afternoon meeting with her pet Landmarks Preservation charity, Gabrielle struck a more formal, professional pose. She simply slicked back her hair into a classic French twist (chignon) and smoothed down stray ends with a little pomade.

During intermission at an opera gala at the Met, the classic line of Gabrielle's basic cut really shone through. She spritzed her hair and then used a blow-dryer and a round brush--one with a larger diameter than Sharon's--to coax in the curves and turn the ends.

Robin is an aspiring actress who meets the heady budget for her acting coach, voice lessons, dance class, and wardrobe by designing inspired arrangements for a fashionable Park Avenue florist. Her day is an intricate wire-walking act, demanding that she play as many roles as she ultimately plans to create on the stage and screen.

Stealing a note from nature on her way to work, Robin had to do little to bring out the natural beauty of her own luxuriant auburn hair. This perennially popular shag cut--air-dried in the morning, tossed a few times, and hand-shaped--simply follows the contours of her head.

With an important afternoon audition coming up, Robin added loads of mousse to her dry hair to create volume, then pulled it up and behind one ear with a pretty comb (she could just as easily have used a bobby pin). This accentuated her lovely bone structure.

Now Robin's ambitious dreams become reality as she prepares for her first important off-Broadway role in *The Little Foxes*. Extravagance is the mode here, and it couldn't be easier. Robin just brushes through her hair to unstiff it, rolls it over and up, secures it with bobby pins, and adds a black velvet bow as a contrast to her glorious Titian tresses. Because this is a shag cut, the top and crown hair are not caught in the roll but are splendidly shown off with the side and back hair tucked away. High drama indeed!

Phoebe is a young comet rising in the star-studded firmament of book publishing. From reading unsolicited manuscripts at slave wages, she has capitalized on her sure instinct for nurturing talented writers to reach the upper echelons. Literary agents love her, and she has just landed her first major title, associate publisher at one of New York's prestige publishing houses.

Phoebe's day moves at the speed of light from aerobics class to editorial meeting, to lunch with a literary power broker, conferences with important authors and on to the Literary Guild glitziana at the St. Regis.

First thing in the morning, sky high on aerobic energy, Phoebe headed for her Chelsea apartment to dress for work. Even very straight hair, if cut right, will be lively if left to dry on its own. Vigorous finger-combing provided body and bounce. Her streaked hair caught light as she picked her way home through the puddles.

Reflecting the sleek chic of her lunchtime rendezvous, The Four Seasons, Phoebe simply dampened her hair with spritz, and then smoothed it back with pomade. Her dramatic sculpture cut achieved that elusive amalgam of elegance and sheer sexiness.

One of publishing's premiere perks is celebrity-studded parties. For the Guild gala Phoebe washed her hair (pomaded hair can be recalcitrant), then used her blow-dryer at the roots to create a petaled effect. Then back to pomade--tiny amounts scrunched into the ends to lend brilliance. Let the hot gossip and *bon mots* begin!

Renee's life may bear a surface resemblance to the comfortable quotidian of the suburban housewife's. But like most of the multifaceted women who come to our salon, Renee specializes in the subtle art of the unexpected. Her days are as full as the busiest of my high-powered women executives.

Though it's not yet ten A.M., Renee has worked out vigorously with Jane Fonda on her videocassette recorder, and is enjoying a respite with her coffee and the *Times*.

Renee has chosen the perfect haircut for her unfolding life. Just as she's grown her two kids out of the nest, her interests to encompass graduate degrees in psychology and literature, and

her marriage to that elusive silver anniversary, Renee is growing out her hair. After years of coloring, she is contemplating a return to her *roots*. This means keeping her hair in mint condition, so she has simply cleaned and conditioned it, using the scalp massage styling technique.

Returning from a late afternoon appointment at my salon, Renee had had an intensive lesson in the exquisitely simple art of hands-on styling.

Swathed in silver fox for that special evening with her husband at the country club, Renee was transformed. Like the intricate interplay of black and silver in her coat, her hair reflected a shimmering chiaroscuro of light and dark.

Renee has mastered the major magic--how to make an ally out of that old nemesis who kept her prisoner for so long--her hair. Renee has been set free.

Split Ends

A WOMAN'S LIFE WITH HER HAIR

RICHARD STEIN

PHOTOGRAPHY BY DAVID TURNER

About the Author

Emphasis on elegance and individuality has made RICHARD STEIN an internationally recognized innovator in hair cutting, styling, and re-imaging. Since he began his career in London's finest Mayfair beauty salons, his trend setting ideas have been matched by his concern for hair health and natural care. A multifaceted artist, Stein engages in a variety of creative pursuits, including writing music and lyrics, sculpting, and acting. He is the author of Set Free:The Book About Hair published by Simon & Schuster, 1988. Originally from the United Kingdom, Mr. Stein currently resides in Manhattan, New York.

Split Ends

A WOMAN'S LIFE WITH HER HAIR

By RICHARD STEIN

Table of Contents

INTRODUCTION BY RICHARD STEIN

HAIR AND RELATIONSHIP
Cut Down to Size by Phyllis Rose
A History of Hair by Elizabeth Lapin
The Hair by Diane Ackerman

HAIR AND GLAMOUR
An Expression of Self by Mia Rae Benenate

HAIR AND HUMOR
Detachments by Marjorie Rosen
Hair Today ... by Emily Colas

HAIR AND HEALTH
To Climb, Ascend, Descend, Transcend by Janet Sternburg

HAIR AND GRACE
The Hairs by Sharon Olds
The Problem of the Mirror by Louise Gluck
Why I Went Gray Over My Summer Vacation by Dr. Ruth K. Westheimer

INTRODUCTION
Richard Stein

My career as a hairdresser began for me in London in the early sixties. I was a Cockney kid who had gained entree into the glamorous world of the Mayfair beauty salon as an apprentice. It was a most exhilarating time and place. London was swinging and at the same time poised to become the fashion influence for the world. Hairdressers like Vidal Sassoon (one of my most important mentors) were opening the door for kids like me to become part of the growing beauty industry. By the time I was seventeen I was already a successful hairdresser. I was eighteen when I was offered the chance to work in New York City and there I have made my home these many years. My success in London followed me to America.

In addition to my work in the salon, I found great opportunities here for a study program that I had created for myself. I delved deeply into music, art, literature, and metaphysics and found in them rich material that synchronized with attending to people's beauty needs. The two pursuits, hairdressing and my personal study program, amplified one another perfectly. The beauty salon was the natural place for me to bring the ideas I was studying and to create another level in my daily work experience. It became clearer and clearer to me that how one presents oneself in the world physically is intrinsically linked to one's inner state.

Over the years I have observed that something magical happens in beauty salons as women talk about their hair or their make-up or their clothing. When there is empathy rather than competitiveness, trust begins to grow. For years, I've witnessed this magical "something" in my salon as women share their hopes and fears, their successes and their disappointments, their triumphs and their failures. The salon then becomes transformed from a place where one comes to be beautified into a haven of safe and relaxed conversation.

Beauty salons began to appear in the early 1900s and catered to women from varying backgrounds. Here, women who might not otherwise have made contact, enjoyed a new-found freedom to connect. Feminism, an extraordinarily wonderful movement, thrived in this milieu and I am proud to have witnessed some part of it and to have been an active supporter.

When I opened my salon in 1972, it was the first salon to openly service men and women in Manhattan. Astonishingly, up until then, it was actually illegal for men to frequent women's salons although, paradoxically, women were permitted in the barbershop. Today, the beauty salon is a uni-sex environment -even, you might say, a uni-sex event. Men and women now meet each other safely in the salon and watch each other being dyed, permed, or teased without embarrassment, and certainly with less vanity. It has become increasingly obvious to me that hair plays an extraordinarily important part both in the way we view ourselves and the way others view us. The psychological impact of hairstyle in terms of self-esteem and self-image is powerful. Yet there is so little written, so few resources available, to help us understand this intricate and complex issue. In response to the paucity of material about hair in all its ramifications, prompted the idea for this book. It is an idea that has generated much excitement. When I invited some of the women whose hair I style to contribute to this book of prose and poetry, the response was enthusiastic and, I must say heart-warming. Women who write for other women can promote the healing of the split ends of distorted attitudes that have arisen. For that, perhaps, a fresh perspective on the multi-dimensional subject of hair will emerge.

I hoped to create an atmosphere of face-to-face, across the table conversation with these women. Hearing their personal stories and making an emotional connection, even for a brief moment in time, gives me a deep sense of gratitude to the participants' generosity and willingness to allow me into their lives.

HAIR AND RELATIONSHIP
Richard Stein

*I*t's conceivable that having a healthy relationship with our hair, understanding the spectrum of possibilities in its texture, color, and style and how it affects us and others, is of primary importance in the overall effect of our constantly changing personal appearance.

Over the years as a working stylist, I have witnessed countless clients' hair obsessions and distresses about their tresses. It has made me keenly aware of just how important it is to have one's hair be on target at all times. I am also truly convinced that there is an intimate connection between one's outer appearance and one's inner world, i.e., healthy self-image, self-confidence, and the ability to perform well in life.

Hair can rule. I remember one client with particularly fine hair telling me a poignantly funny story. She had met a terrific guy shortly after her divorce. They had dated and painted the town hot pink.. This was at a time when hairpieces, known as "falls," were in vogue. All through the dating period, painfully insecure about her fine hair, she had worn one to give it the illusion of fullness. Never mind that she'd had to anchor the fall to the crown of her head with a thousand thorny bobby pins. When the moment finally came for sexual encounter, the poor woman was traumatized. *To wear or lose the wiglet?* Finally deciding to keep it on, she proceeded to spend what could have been a grand time worrying about the hairpiece instead of letting go and enjoying herself. She had traded ego for orgasm. That relationship quickly deteriorated, but she pulled out the bobby pins and went on to meet and many someone who appreciated her with her own hair. True love after the fall!

It's probably a sweeping generalization that men have practically no understanding whatsoever of a woman's hair agenda, (or very little of their own, for that matter), but it's certainly what I've witnessed over the years. The atmosphere in a glitzy beauty salon is dramatically different from the no-nonsense masculinity of the old-fashioned barbershop. With the advent of the unisex salon in the mid-1970s, born when wives and girl friends began bringing their attendant males in to be styled by her beautician, men have not-so-stealthily invaded the sanctorum of feminine privacy. The veil has been lifted. Voyagers of "the beauty secret," men can now catch glimpses of their significant other and lots of other women being dyed, highlighted, lip-waxed, and pedicure... not at their burnished best. (No good deed goes unpunished!) Small compensation that women can watch the uneasy males struggle with their own, only recently, often dimly-perceived, style needs.

Men have complained bitterly and perennially to their womenfolk about the amount of time, paraphernalia and energy spent on "doing their hair." Perhaps this is one of those basic bargains in a relationship, like who gets to do the washing up or walk the dog. The "hair issue" between couples is often just such a trade-off -she gets to spend outrageous amounts of money, time, and energy on her hair with hair dyes, other products, and marathon visits to the beauty parlor -all in the name of pleasing him. He, in turn, gets to avoid diet and exercise and continue to smoke his wretched cigars. A woman friend recently confessed to me, after a long and bitter divorce, that for all the years of the marriage, her former husband had been cutting her hair, albeit with no formal training. She had hated it but it was loath to upset him by telling him so. How's that for unspoken agreements?

Then there's the complex interplay between hair and a person's relation to their larger cosmos and their fellow travelers in it. Most people rely on hairstylists or friends to give them an opinion about their hair because they understand little or nothing of its nature or style potential. They are the hair *fashionistas*, addicted to the quick fix of the "hairdo of the day." Movie stars, models, and celebrities are the style bellwethers for a public avid for a *new look* at their cost, never mind that it may have nothing whatsoever to do with their own faces, bodies, or hair. Peer pressure has its place in this equation, too. I've often wondered whether women try harder to impress their women friends in the style department, than they do their significant male others. Here's where the hair/self-image part becomes blurry, and a women tries to please everyone, losing focus of her own needs. Then, there's pure hair perversity -with women wanting the diametric opposite of what they have straight or curly -and so spending a great deal of time, energy, and money trying to achieve the improbable.

The relationship between hairdresser and client is an intricate one. Hairdressers play many roles and represent different things to different people -confidante, confessor, parent, relative, therapist, and on and on. A world-famous psychiatrist used to tell me that sitting in my salon waiting to get a haircut, listening carefully to all the various conversations swirling around her, she'd heard things being discussed that would have taken *years* to be revealed to her in her practice. Not all hairdresser/client relationships have an immediate "chemistry;" most have to be worked on and developed over time. As in all relationships, listening empathically to each other is key. I personally view each individual as a work in progress, which enables me to create a viable style agenda -a kind of personal database of styles that I use and can constantly hone and refer to over our collaboration.

It is hard for a hairdresser not to get personally involved with his or her client. The physical intimacy of the "laying on of scissors" and the close proximity of chair to stylist make it almost an inevitability. Over time, a friendship usually evolves, and mutual information is exchanged that can be, by turns, revealing and potentially embarrassing. I've been fortunate in attracting a large and eclectic clientele over the years, many interesting and important people coming from diverse walks of life. Even though I did not take an "oath of silence," I have always felt an obligation to maintain a low gossip profile, being careful not to indulge or divulge and keeping the focus where it belongs, on the creative part.

However, given all the perils intrinsic to the situation, the mutual benefits surely outweigh the risks. The exchange of information that takes place on all levels -conversation, good feelings, and the "new look" -can be transcendental for both parties. I call it the "beauty agreement." Many times when I have finished doing someone's hair, they leave my chair with a different sense of themselves -and with their mood elevated without recourse to Prozac. I believe that special, upbeat mood change is deserved... that it is part of the beauty salon experience, part of the promise. People will go to great lengths -travel far and pay a great deal of money for it. I have always tried to acknowledge and honor my partnership in this intangible beauty agreement.

Endings are often an inevitable, often painful part of relationships, and especially so in the volatile beauty business. Hairdressers move from salon to salon like planets in their spheres, as do their clients, orbiting from stylist to stylist. Certainly at this juncture, in Manhattan, circa A.D. 2000, there is very little sense of loyalty in the community. This lack of permanence ultimately affects the stylist's attitude to the ever-shifting scene, and hence the client. Being able to let go of clients when the moment comes is as important as keeping them close until that time. I have always believed in an open door attitude, so that people can leave and return comfortable -and they do!

Cut Down to Size
Phyllis Rose

Once I tried to find a hairdresser less expensive than the one I usually use. Calling in August, I got an appointment in late October. My hair grew. Ends split. Eventually I drove the two hours from my home in Manhattan.

My appointment was for noon. I changed into the salon smock and read a magazine. At 12:05, the receptionist told me that Roger had called on his car phone: stuck in traffic, he would be a little late.

He was only fifteen minutes late. Richard regularly kept me waiting half an hour, sometimes an hour, with no apology. If Roger got in his car and circled the block in order to call a new client on the car phone and put her in a state of abjection, he needn't have bothered. I felt abject as all get-out in that awful smock, my hair almost as blond as a Barbie doll's and seeming both to frizz and hang limply to mid-neck.

Roger said, "Too bad you've changed. I like to see my clients in their own clothes first, to get a sense of their style." A good-looking man with blue eyes and dark hair, he eyed me with distaste. "But I must tell you, I'd be very surprised if I end up cutting your hair."

That, I supposed, was a joke, so I joked in return: "My clothes are hanging in the closet. You can take a look at them if you like."

"Good idea," he said solemnly. I led him to my clothes. He looked, and then, like a young knight in a fairy tale required to make love to a hideous hag, brought me to his chair before the mirror.

I said, "Judith suggested I come to you." "Judith's hair is typical of the work I do."

"I like Judith's hair. That's why I'm here."

"Judith's hair is healthy."

"Oh, I see," I said. "You're not into damaged hair."

"No," he said, holding a strand or two of my hair distantly, as though it were blue spaghetti. "I'm not. Overworked color like yours -well, I only like it when it's intended to be amusing. We might have tried to bring it back, but you've taken it too far. I'd be very surprised if I could cut your hair. Didn't you come in for a consultation? That's why I like to do consultations."

"No one said anything about a consultation. I've waited three months for this appointment." Tears were coming to my eyes, and I had no privacy. There were clients on my left and right and hairdressers at work on them, pretending not to listen. "I drove two hours to get here."

He said, 'Well, we'll wash out your conditioner" -pronounced to mean inferior, second-rate product - "and see what we have then."

I summoned up my last bit of self-esteem and said, "It doesn't sound as if it's worth the trouble. You don't seem to like anything about my hair."

"No," said Roger, "I don't." And so I walked out, and managed not to start crying until I hit Seventh Avenue.

The French have a phrase to describe the things you should have said but didn't have the presence of mind to say at the time, the things you thought of as you left the scene of confrontation -*l'esprit d'escalier*, staircase wit. Many friends later helped me come to terms with my humiliation by contributing pieces of staircase wit. "Who do you think you are? Picasso?" was a favorite. The best from a man who refused to believe that Roger liked women, and I will give only an expurgated version: "If you think this is bad, you should see me naked."

My mother, who is old school and thinks of hair-dressers as servants and employees rather than artists and professionals, was horrified that I took this insult from an "underling." What kind of spineless creature had she spawned? Another friend echoed her: "Who would have thought you were so passive?"

Most of my friends seemed to think they could have handled it better than I did, and I'm sure they were right. One insinuated that it served me right for being so elitist as to go to New York to get my hair cut. However much it shook my confidence, the incident did me no harm with my acquaintances. Envy is the only dangerous feeling to provoke. Giving people a chance to patronize you every once in a while only increases their affection.

I saw a woman humiliated by a hairdresser in Paris. It wasn't a pretty sight. I saw her come into the salon proud, strong, self-confident, and leave like a whipped dog. An American, she had come to Paris all the way from Germany, where she was living, because she didn't trust the Germans to do her hair.

She had grown it for years so that it could be cut straight across the bottom, as was being done in New York. The Parisian hairdresser began to layer it. The proud woman winced and tried to object. The hairdresser said, "I cannot cut your hair unless you have confidence in me." After that, the woman quivered and watched without protest as her hair was ruined. When the hairdresser stepped away for a moment, she broke into tears and I tried to comfort her. We both agreed that the worst part was, French women looked good. Why couldn't we?

At that moment I realized what a complex cultural achievement a haircut is, the product not only of a sophisticated negotiation between hairdresser and client, but of subtle, culturally coded understandings of identity and status. As an American, I could see this was a woman to be reckoned with, but the French hairdresser did not. Treated as though she were contemptible, she soon became so.

The haircut I got that day was equally poor. Later I learned from a journalist friend what I had to do to get my hair cut well in Paris. I had to explain very carefully that I was a writer and that I wanted *un-look Colette*. Otherwise the hairdresser, unable to place me, would do a second-rate assembly line haircut.

I think that no man would stand for the treatment from a barber that women get from hairdressers. Perhaps the low-cost haircut is men's secret source of strength. I know a very successful lawyer who likes to go to the cheap barbers in Grand Central Terminal with moral fervor, as thought to give in to the pressures to get an eighty-dollar haircut were to begin down a path that leads inevitably to insider trading. He may be right.

For women, however, I would argue that moral strength lies on the side of the expensive -or at any rate abusive -haircut. My experience with Roger is the kind that keeps you humble, makes you a kinder person, prevents you from misusing your own power, holds arrogance at bay. If the seven-dollar haircut and its attendant humiliations keep well-heeled women attuned to the plight of the scorned and unfortunate.

The afternoon of my humiliation by Roger, I was lucky enough to get an appointment with my darling Richard. He ran his fingers unhesitatingly through my bleached-out strands and said, "I love your hair." "You do? Really?" I said, with pathetic gratitude. I would never try to leave him again. I would put up with his little weaknesses, like charging too much. "Yes, I really love it," he said. I should have been reassured, my ego re-inflated, but instead I said to myself, "Richard must be into damaged hair."

Phyllis Rose is the author of *Woman of Letters: A Life of Virginia Wolff, Parallel Lives: Five Victorian Marriages, Writing of Women: Essays in a Renaissance, Jazz Cleopatra: Josephine Baker in Her Time, Never Say Goodbye: Essays*, and the editor of *The Norton Book of Women's Lives*.

A History of Hair
Elizabeth Lapin

Cut, snip, yes
snip, snip, cut, they fought. One brief moment,
in a family-made reel, I am
whirling, and my hair
swims in the air, like the near Pacific.

My hands bend,
Turn and retreat. I am myself, then.

The rest of time, I am stepping down
the Beverly Hills library steps carrying books
held on top by my chin. My chair is a scholarly, crisp
bun nailed to the nape of my neck.

At five, my mother laid me on the butcher block
and with the toothed bread-knife
started to saw the hair.
She cursed and damned, the snares and snarls.
I got to make things easy, baby.

My hair was too much for her.
she took me to Danny's **Snip and Curl.**
Close to the head, like my son, she said.
I fell to the floor of Danny's shop
screaming, *Give it back.*
In small white, bags meant for lollipops and barrettes,
I gathered up my hair.
I think I may have looked strange on my hands and knees
with bristled head, gathering myself.
She can't be in the picture shows, now, my father screamed.

He fell in love with the beehive lady and
fled the house
forever – mostly, I think, because of hair.

Mother, still beautiful at 61,
has grey and black fierce hair
falling to her buttocks.
She straightens every day between the heated tongs.
Down and up, she clamps
away the curls and waves,
I've never seen her hair as it would have been.

Except once while she was sweeping the leaves
I took a garden hose to her.
The screen door slammed.
Wetted down she disappeared
into the house with her sudden charges of tangled, wiry strands.
For years I was kept inside, forbidden to leave
until the hair wound on plastic rollers
had smoothed out. *I don't want to look at you.*
No one wants to look at you, she said.
My stepfather would hold my hair like hundreds of trinkets in his hand.

After a month of my father's death
my mother far away in Missouri said, *How's*
your hair? I replied, *a mess.* I meant a mass of mourning.
Then don't come home for the holiday.

On the floor in the Auschwitz museum a ton or so of hair reaching to the ceiling,
thousands of tons stored in Polish warehouses, museums, and barns.
Heaps of brown, black, red, glistening fresh hair,

in a glass tank telescoping to the ceiling, all freshly washed.

I made my first vow to never cut again.
my Jewish hair. The hair on lips, toes, in my nose,
legs, thighs, arms, underarms, between buttocks,
around belly button, between my legs.
In Auschwitz with a prayer shawl wrapped around them men lived
exactly six months longer than they did without one;
the springing hair became my prayer shawl.

I wanted to rescue the hair, put it back on the heads,
I wanted to spread prayer shawls over the bodies of the murdered, before
they were murdered.

Mother, I want to give you a gift of my prayer shawl,
my hair, all of it, in a suitcase
with my name **Lapin-Rudolph** painted
white like other suitcases on
on display in the room next door,
which were painted with the names
of friends from Sunday School class;
Kahn, Eliasberg, Levy, Cohen, Jacob, Tuchman, and **Goodman.**

Each line I write is like a strand of my hair.
They are to go into ears and come out of mouths.
Your tongue licked me straight up.
Was all that stacked-up hair a huge pile of German sentences?
Now I see that everything is hair: butterflies, ferns,
canoes, onion skin, lily pods, bee's wings, sand.
What isn't hair.

The Hair
Diane Ackerman

When lovers describe their sweethearts, they usually mention the color and length of their hair. One may love the whole person, body, and spirit, but hair becomes the fetish of that love. Yielding and soft, sumptuous and colorful, decorative, and dangling, it invites a lover's touch. It's fun to fondle, play with, and disarrange. Messing it up is the symbolic equivalent of undressing the other's body. A woman quickly learns that cutting her hair without warning her lover first is a bad mistake. Even a becoming change of hairstyle can be shocking and disturbing.

A boyfriend, on the verge of breaking up with me, once exclaimed with a wince, "Your hair!" "What's wrong with it?" I asked, suddenly vulnerable as a trembling fawn. 'Well, there's just so much of it ..." he said. I knew then that everything was over between us. Hair is the caressable plumage of love, a feature individual as the shape of one's chin or the size of one's fingers. If he had said: "I no longer like your mouth," it wouldn't have been more wounding. I once tucked a perfect curl of my hair, tied with a lavender ribbon, between the pages of a poetry book I was returning to a friend. The curl marked my favorite love poem, and I felt as if I were charging the book with my life force. I knew I was giving him a powerful talisman. Hair is sacred to lovers, but also to society.

In the late sixties, a white woman was nowhere if she didn't have straight hair. Straight hair suggested a non-ethnic (and therefore upper-class) bloodline; the cheerleaders all wore their blond hair straight. And among the rebels who yearned to be like Judy Collins and Joan Baez, it expressed a sincerity based on contempt for society, hand-me-down values, and the coiffed generation's ideals. However, I came into this world capped in black curly hair -deep-night black with real corkscrew curls -and you could no more straighten it than you could hold back the sea. But I tried. I used to iron my hair; get it temporarily denatured in a reverse permanent; or set it on jumbo orange-juice cans. In fact, most of my teen years were spent sleeping on rollers of one Inquisitional design or another. "Beauty sleep" was the oxymoron. What self-imposed tyranny! For short spells, my hair did look "tamed," "tidy," "controlled." Society was exploding in all directions, but my hair was in place. Lack of control was scary, and suggested the lawlessness of murder, bank robbery, or having sex -all equally criminal for "nice girls" when I was sixteen.

Then, sweet miracle, one day many years later I walked into the Lexington Avenue salon of Richard Stein, whose pretty, vivacious styles I had seen on a number of fashionable women. He looked compassionately at my country-western hairdo, which had taken two hours under a hair dryer to achieve, and said indignantly on my behalf: "Why do you do this to yourself?" Then he turned the animal in my hair loose, shaping it into a long thick shag -the waterfall of curls it always yearned for -and for the first time in my life I had simple, wash-and-wear hair. The years of setting, drying, and vanity-rich fussing were over. So was a special kind of bondage to one rigid ideal of beauty. A symbolic freedom came from accepting my hair on its own terms, relishing its eccentricities instead of trying to disguise them. Now, once every three months or whenever I begin to feel like a sheepdog, Richard tames what he refers to as my "Queen of the Amazon" hair. He has often been the last person I would see before setting out on an expedition, or the first when I returned. This does not surprise him. Scissorwise and insightful, he knows well how symbolic hair is, particularly to women.

And especially for me, since my hair sometimes seems to have a life of its own. "Just look for a weather system of black hair," I say, "and you'll find me." A poetry student of mine (who was also a professional cartoonist) once did a series of drawings about a woman with my kind of hair. It was her hair that a beau introduced to his parents, her hair that chose from a menu, her hair that streamed out of a car window like Spanish moss. Recently, when I was having the house enlarged to accommodate a room that's combination bathroom and astronomical observatory (one telescope), a twinkling-eyed woman whose job it was to help design that sensory marvel, said: "I don't know what your taste is ...but I presume it's like your hair." Then she suggested a harem tent fluttering over the tub, its flight propelled by small strategically placed fans. Once, stricken by despair, I phoned a girlfriend and, when I calmed down enough to speak, sobbed out my woes. "Oh, boy trouble," she said in a tone of voice that meant *Hell, we can deal with that*. "I was afraid you'd got a bad haircut." When her daughter was born, she cradled the baby in her arms and swore: "I promise I'll never give you a hard time about how you wear your hair."

This is the crux of the matter. Mothers and daughters are always confronting each other on the battlefield of a daughter's hair. I know so many women whose mothers would greet them -sometimes before even saying hello -by pushing their hair straight back and exclaiming, "You'd look so much better with the hair off your face, dear!" They say this for years, regardless of how hairstyles change, and it's always accompanied by yanking the hair back severely, as if it should be held by an Ace bandage.

It's as if a daughter were seen as the incarnation of the pure side of a mother's being. An important moment comes when a mother tells her daughter that she likes her hairdo, which often occurs late in life and signals an armistice of larger dimensions. There is something too sexy about out-of-control hair, or hair falling over the face. Something too competitive. Remember how Glenn Close in the movie *Fatal Attraction* is always seen with psychotic blue eyes under a blond whitewater of hair. When long haired women have children, they frequently cut their hair short. Pleading convenience, they explain it merely as a practical move. But it is, I think, more symbolic. In various cultures and religions (among nuns and some Jewish, for instance) women are expected to cut their hair short so that they will no longer be attractive to men. A freshly bobbed new mother might be saying, in essence, I'm going to focus my life now on nurturing my family; I'm not available for flirtation. At the end of World War II, collaborators were de-sexed and shamed by having their hair chopped off in what was, essentially, a form of social circumcision. Mothers often wish a daughter to cut hers short when she reaches puberty, but fathers want a daughter to keep her hair long forever,. A friend tells me that when she turned fourteen her mother talked her into cutting her waist-length hair, much to the horror of her father who, in a melodramatic and ritual symbolic gesture, insisted that he alone be allowed to cut it.

   Throughout history, hair has been considered not just ornamental but magical. In ancient Egypt, a widow would bury a lock of her hair with her husband as a charm and, possibly, as a vow that her love went with him. The goddess Isis used her hair as a rejuvenating fabric to bestow life on her dead lover, Osiris; and even the shadow of her hair, spread like the wings of an eagle, protected her child from harm. The constellation Bernice's hair -a pretty cascade of stars lying between Boötes and Leo -is said to be the hair of an Egyptian queen who lived in the third century B.C. and was married to her brother, Ptolemy III Euergetes. Soon after the wedding, Ptolemy III went off to war in Asia, and Bernice swore that if he returned alive and victorious she would sacrifice her hair to the gods. I don't think her motive was that the gods needed chignons, but the all-too-human belief that nothing good happens without the requisite amount of sacrifice or punishment. On Ptolemy's safe return, she offered up her long hair in the temple of Aphrodite near present-day Aswan. but the next day, mysteriously, the hair vanished. Soon the Alexandrian mathematician and astronomer, Conon of Samos, alerted the king to a swarm of stars he had seen near the tail of the constellation Leo, and his conviction that they were the queen's hair, set in the heavens to commemorate Ptolemy's victory. What really happened to Bernice's hair, we will never know. (Perhaps Conon secretly had a crush on Bernice, and wanted at least to possess her hair, an intimate par of her.) But its discovery certainly was timely.

Although I haven't always been happy with my hair, I never thought of it as literally demonic. Now and then I might have hoped it would beguile, but I didn't suppose it was supernaturally evil, the devil's circuitry, the whips of hell. In more superstitious days, however, people associated horror with women's hair. During the Middle Ages, the unruly hair of "witches" was thought to control the weather. All manner of hail, hurricanes, or windstorms could be unleashed by a woman allowing her hair to fall wild. Of course there was always some woman somewhere who didn't give a fig for the reputed evil in her hair, and unbraided her long tresses to have a good wash. This was considered highly uncivic-minded, since, as everyone knew, a thunderstorm occurred solely because a woman somewhere was combing out her hair. In Corinthians 11:10, St. Paul warns that good Christian women should cover their heads because demons leap like sparks from female hair and enter the world to do mischief. The tradition of a woman covering her head in church originated with this belief, that any mild-mannered woman could poison the church building with her lice-like demons.

Pagan superstitions about hair ran riot during the Middle Ages. One example: bury a snippet of hair from a menstruating witch and it will become a snake. Reminiscent of the Medus myth, this one combines many suggestive images -witches, the temptation of Eve, the supposed filthiness of menstruation, the power that came from secretly possessing a lock of someone's hair. But there was also good magic associated with hair, especially when strands were braided and given as amulets. Lovers often exchange locks of hair, and knights rode to battle with a precious twist of their lady's sacred hair to keep them brave.

But hair symbolized more than romance; it can also serve as a political placard. Each generation, needing to feel a sense of identity, sets itself apart through hairstyle. Because there are only so many things one can do with one's hair to shock society, styles seem to reappear after a decade or so. Those who lived through love-ins and antiwar rallies probably find it as strange as I do to see construction workers now wearing ponytails and headbands or a policeman with long sideburns. Or a corporate man in a conservative suit wearing a ponytail. It makes me do a double take: the look is hippie, but the politics and philosophy are different. History, myth, and literature are filled with dramas in which hair plays a central role. Most often it symbolizes strength, as in the story of Samson and Delilah; or sexuality, as in the fairy tale about Rapunzel; or selfless love, as in the famous short story by O. Henry; or fetish magic, as in American Indian lore; or a religious portent, as in the Aztec myth from which Cortes profited -that a god would appear from afar and be recognizable by his blond hair. I won't argue that hair brought down the monarchy in eighteenth-century France, but it may have helped to focus society's rage. At Marie Antoinette's court, both men and women were said to use barrels of flour to whiten their elaborate wigs. Reputedly, this waste so outraged the common people, who were starving for want of bread, that they cut their own hair short in protest and, ultimately, condemned royal hair and heads to the guillotine.

Merely thinking about the eighteenth century's huge, cloud-like wigs and the matted, rarely washing hair beneath makes my skin crawl. I like to wash my hair every day, unless I'm far from running water. At times, I go on expeditions into perfect wilderness. Then I braid my hair, leaving my fluffy bangs loose. Yet my hair sometimes disturbs male scientists enough they feel obliged to comment on it. For example, when I was making arrangements for a recent trip to the Brazilian rain forest, the project director took a hard look at me and said, "You'll have to do something with your hair." "I can pull it back," I assured him, trying not to smile. Most people understand the concept of long hair -that it can be braided, put in a ponytail, or in other ways subdued for hot weather or dense foliage. But he instinctively remarked on it, as others in his position sometimes have, because long hair is suggestive. It implies excess, extravagance, rampant sensuality -literally, a lack of restraint. Expedition work tends to be unisex, and it's tough to work efficiently if there are man/woman distractions and complications. So people are often fearful of accentuating gender differences by wearing sexy clothes and loose hair, of setting free the "demons" of temptation.

The same seems to be true on the electronic frontier. These past years, which much hoopla, four of network television's anchorwomen bobbed their hair. What I find fascinating is all the ruckus it caused. Deborah Norville, then of the *Today* show, said: "My hair was never my own on television." After her *20/20* interview with Boris Yeltsin, Barbara Walters received compliments, but she was amazed to find that some were just about her new haircut. There is a tacit assumption in the media that long hair looks vampy, not authoritative or sincere, and that changing the length of hair changes the sexual message. It also changes the sexual message at home. "Now I have a whole new life," Diane Sawyer, of *PrimeTime Live*, said to Newsweek, "I do a year doing investigative reporting, and you call about my hair!" Her husband is reported to have complained that he went to bed with a sex symbol and "woke up with Peter Pan."

Human lovers aren't the only ones fixated on hair. Other primates devote a lot of time to mutual nitpicking and grooming -not just for cleanliness but as a way to weave relationships. Most mammals adore mutual preening. Perhaps that's why we can fuss wIth a loved one's hair for hours in a state of hypnotic rapture. Hair care is a task one rarely performs alone. We require others to tend our hair at beauty salons. We obsessively prepare our hair for our loved ones. Yet hair is not the most vital part of us. It shimmers and moves, but it composed of dead cells. We may harvest it from time to time, carve or color it, but it will grow again and return to its weedy ways. In this, it echoes the sheer disarray of nature. People so often complain that their hair to is "wild," that they "can't do anything with it," that it's nothing but "split ends" and "strays," that it's hopelessly "fly-away." Perhaps we fear that, like ourselves, and like our feelings of love, despite our constant efforts, it will always be just a little bit out of control.

Diane Ackerman is the author of *A Natural History of the Senses, Twilight of the Tenderfoot, On Extended Wings, The Moon by Whale Light*, and five collections of poems, *The Planets: A Cosmic Pastoral, Wife of Light, Lady Faustua, Reverse Thunder: A Dramatic Poem*, and *Jaguar of Sweet Laughter: New and Selected Poems*. She has received the Academy of American Poets' Peter I.B. Lavan Award, and grants from the National Endowment for the Arts and the Rockefeller Foundation.

Reprinted with permission from **A Natural History of the Love**, *Random House, 1994.*

HAIR AND GLAMOUR
Richard Stein

It's fairly safe to say that what is considered glamorous in both hair and clothing in the 2000's is something of a crapshoot. If there was ever a time of "anything goes," it's now. Ever since the 1960s there has been an extraordinary acceleration in the beauty and fashion world; styles have changed with dizzying velocity, evolving as rapidly as the insatiable media has expanded to chronicle them. Inevitably, this has led to mass confusion, as well as an uncertainty about what style really is.

Each period has its own brand of glamour -the Egyptians and their hennaed coifs, the Greeks with their carefully arranged curls, the Persians with their oiled and glossy ringlets. In 18th century France on the eve of Revolution, some of the towering wigs worn by the aristocracy had birdcages, cunningly concealed within where charming linnets twittered the nights away. And, in London, that ardent Whig and fashion arbiter, the Duchess of Devonshire, boldly sported three, three-foot ostrich feathers, the emblem of her lover, the Prince of Wales. All through history, hair has reflected the times. The Puritans fanatically anti-glamour -shunned all artifice, hence hair was usually cropped, covered, and hidden. Clearly, they knew the fierce temptation of the toss of a saucy curl. Certainly the flapper bobs of the 1920s helped liberate a lot of women to raise hell and their hemlines, in direct defiance of the primly prurient Victorian era that went before.

My own ideas of glamour grew out of my admiration for the hairstyles of the very silent movies on up until the mid-1940s. My work methods are a homage to the way great stars like Greta Garbo, Joan Crawford, Bette Davis, Gloria Swanson and others wore their hair. They were innovators of classic and timeless effects, with their "looks" that celebrated the independent, feminine woman. They lived at a time when an actor created a special look for each role played, unlike today when armies of stylists follow a star's every move, ready to fluff, advise and critique at the drop of a comb. These women were in a continual process of self-invention and reinvention, active participants in their own styles. They were glamour personified.

Whatever the elements are that conspire to create the illusion called glamour, in today's world "hair rules." Understanding its dynamics and the effect it has on us and the world at large is crucial. A woman's visual statement starts at the top. One's hair is what is seen first, so the head should always feel in balance and harmony with its hairstyle, whether the body is dressed in a relaxed and casual mode or in glittering haute couture. A quick glance at any nearby mirror is infinitely more reassuring if one's hair has a sense of order, whether the style is high tousle or cutting-edge geometric. Glamour can be in the swing of the hair, or the shine or the natural quality of the cut. Not all hair needs to be conditioned or moussed or colored, despite the siren call of the giddy profusion of hair products on the market today. It should always feel good to the wearer's touch, and when it doesn't is when it's time to move on to a newer look.

I believe a woman's quest for glamour begins in the morning and builds throughout the day, as she anticipates the evening with its demand for high style and high excitement. Maybe one artful flick of a curl can change a mood and a mode and prepare her for the nighttime drama ahead. A friend recently confided to me that, just taking an extra twenty minutes a day to work with her hair in different ways, frees her from the need for makeup! Having found a new confidence in her hair craft, may also provide her the courage to try a new wardrobe or fragrance.

Glamour is ultimately in the eye of the beholder, and it has no single, accessible secret. It is allure, charm, fascination, with just a hint of witchery. It is art and artifice and alchemy. No "glamour.com" site exists to guide the novice in its wily ways. Acquiring it takes personal daring and the connivance of inspired and sympathetic experts. It's the whole package -makeup, clothing, accessories and, of course in my view, a brilliant hairstyle. And, quintessentially, it's the *attitude* of the woman who wears them.

AN EXPRESSION OF SELF
Mia Rae Bennate

Why not radiate beauty? If it's possible to show yourself to the world in such a way, then why not? Beauty is, to put it simply, an art form as pure and true as Monet's famous *Lily Pond*.

Some claim that spending a lot of time in front of the mirror is self-consumed or arrogant. But why is this so? There is nothing superficial about trying and succeeding to look good. One does not have to be a Hollywood socialite to want this. Glamour is something that is appealing to everyone.

Hair and the way it can be adorned, dressed up, dressed down, and so on, is an expression of self. To be glamourous is not so much to attain a certain look, but to carry oneself in a way that says, "poised, confident, and dare I say, beautiful." Hair can accentuate this beauty in a way that little else, other than what comes from inside, can. As we all know, there are some women today who have a firm grasp on true glamour such as Madonna. She has a natural beauty that speaks for itself but her numerous hair styles over the years have helped mold her style and indi-viduality as a person quite a bit.

As a young woman growing up in modern America, I have often felt that my hair is my most important accessory. That it could make me or break me. To me, my hair is a direct impression in the very same way a bad handshake can be. That, if in fact, my hair did not look good, there was a devastatingly high chance that my whole "look" would be ruined. It was at times such as this when I had to tell myself sulkily that its not what's on the outside that counts. But honestly, I know this is true, but does anyone believe it? I think not.

As a typical adolescent, my appearance becomes increasingly important. At a point when I was younger; struggling to figure out where I fit in the world, my hair became my biggest problem. If I could just get my hair to look right, everything else would be ok.

I thought I had been unlucky when I was born as far as my hair was concerned. My hair was mousy brown, stringy, always looked dirty, and would not grow past my shoulders. As a result of this, or so I thought, I had many problems. My most vivid memories are of me in front of a mirror desperately attempting to straighten my hair before school. At the time, I was not coordinated with a blow dryer and as a result could never, and I mean never. get my hair to look even close to the way I wanted. So I started to cut off the pieces that I didn't feel looked "right." This became a daily routine and well. you can guess what happened.

Fortunately, I grew up a bit and have realized that the more I grow as a person the better I look physically -hair and all. As I see it, the outside shows who you are on the inside. Bad hair days are allowed and unavoidable. but have you ever had a bad hair day when feeling extremely good about yourself'? I know I haven't.

I found from personal experience that being glamorous and having beautiful hair are one in the same thing. When I do my hair nicely I find that oth-ers are more receptive to me because I am more confident with the way I look and that always helps to improve the attitude I put forth. Some say, "Why not be happy with yourself when you don't look good?" That in itself is fine. I'm not advocating low self-esteem. My point is if you can add one more pretty face to the world or one more beautiful head of hair than do it!

Glamour is like a rhythm. It flows and creates a path. This path depends on the person obviously, but also like a rhythm, it is not something that you can find in a magazine or the sale rack in a department store because it's inside of you. It is individual and unique and most importantly, it's yours.

Mia Rae Benenate is sixteen years old. She is an actress, singer, and writer. She has appeared in the off-broadway smash rock-musical, *Inappropriate* in New York and Los Angeles. She is currently studying at The American Conservatory Theater in San Francisco and attending the College of Marin.

HAIR AND HUMOR
Richard Stein

Most everybody has a funny story to tell about their own hair, usually about some dreadful mishap -a wrong color choice, a major style mistake, an accidental baldness. Over the years in my own work place -a mirrored, spotlit and crowded stage -I have seen daily drama, ranging from "historical to tragical (no pastoral, I'm strictly urban) to comical." I remember years ago, styling actress Madeline Kahn's hair for her role in the movie *Blazing Saddles*. As I finished, I began to massage her scalp and finger-comb her hair into place, a technique I had evolved to go with my sculpt/cutting work. It also helped to relax the client. The salon was abuzz with customers and stylists, when all of a sudden Madeline began to bark loudly. At first it startled me, until I realized that she was simply expressing pure pleasure at what I was doing. Ms. Madeline Kahn in the role of pampered poodle. (Mel Brooks would have been proud of her.)

When I first started out as a young hairdresser in New York, I landed a job on the beauty floor at Henri Bendel's working with a very popular stylist named Paul Mitchell. Paul and I, who had actually met and worked together in London, quickly became good friends and cohorts in what was then one of Manhattan's most elegant salons. As well as being a superb hairdresser, Paul was a brilliant public relations man, coming up with one great idea after another. One summer, he came across a consignment of Dynel "man-made fiber" half-head wigs that inspired a promotion he called "The Beach Wig." The idea was that a woman could slick her hair back and wear the wig to the beach, tying a bandanna around the top half so that she could protect her hair and look good at the same time.

It was a simple enough promo, and it was running smoothly, until it came to Mrs. Stone. Her wig was on special order -either the size or the color was the problem, maybe both. Those were the days when women paid ritual visits to their hairdressers. Week after week, Mrs. Stone would come to get her hair done and ask for her beach wig. She was increasingly urgent about it, especially as the summer was wearing on and it seemed the perfect solution to her curly hair. Finally it arrived and I ceremoniously put it on her head. There it sat -outsize, untrimmed, shaggy -resembling nothing so much as a dead raccoon. There were a few politely-stifled giggles from nearby work stations. Then a tsunami wave of laughter swept the salon. Fortunately, Mrs. Stone -always a terrific sport -laughed the loudest. That was the one wig that never made it to the beach!

   Hair usually makes a statement, but it can even create a diversion. Recently a client told me a delicious story. She and a friend were at a major event in the area near where her country house is. It was a benefit, designed to raise money for a local music society, and the local gentry and not -so-gentry were all in attendance. As she made her way through the bustling crowd, she suddenly spotted the man she had been dating with another woman. It was too late to retrace her steps and avoid being seen -dressed as she was to the conspicuous nines -so she could do nothing but press on. Just as she was about to come face to face with her paramour and his lady friend, a woman stopped her and in a very loud voice exclaimed, "I must tell you I have been admiring your hair all evening. You have the best haircut I've ever seen!" After thanking her admirer, she turned, greeted the couple warmly and made a triumphant exit, her hair having saved the evening and her self-esteem.

Detachments
Marjorie Rosen

An interesting thing has happened to hair: Anything goes. Long or short, green or white, braided or even bald, it's all fine, as long as it suits you.

It wasn't always this way. In the 50s, when I was a girl, whatever your hair type or color, it was wrong. Brown hair was supposed to be blonde; blonde, platinum; straight hair needed to be permed and kinky hair straightened. Women used to visit the beauty parlor every single week, hospital stays and death being no exception. There, their crowning glory would be washed, set, dried under huge metal machines, then tortured into the style of the day. Finally, these "do's" (really *don'ts*) would be lacquered into helmet heads exactly like one another, the ozone layer be damned; at night, they would be preserved for the following day in yards of toilet paper secured with a hair net. A woman could be tossed, buffeted, and whisked away into the perfect storm, but one thing was sure; her hair would never move.

By the early 60s, young women were beginning to challenge such stifling decorum. Still, we all longed to be *au courant*; and toward that end, some of us even ironed our hair straight as a ruled edge in order to achieve the look *du jour*: I will never forget how one friend, born with thick, kinky hair, decided to have it professionally unkinked. At the time, this could only be done in a beauty parlor -they were not yet called "salons" -catering to African-Americans. But the straightening solution, which worked wonders on black heads, was, as it turned out, too strong for hers, and every hair on her head fell out.

My friend, however, was in indomitable spirit, determined not to let baldness ruin her social life. So she bought herself a wig. It was expensive and featured luxurious black curls that had once been on someone else's head, and which, she was convinced, transformed her into Elizabeth Taylor's twin -at a time, you understand, when Liz was still the most glamorous creature on the planet. (The rest of us, of course, teased our friend that she looked more like Liz's poodle.) If I'd been open to valuable life lessons in perseverance and ingenuity (which I was *not*), this classmate would have taught me well. After all, she had the presence of mind to tie a colorful babushka over her wig, as much to make sure her store-bought hair didn't fall off her head when she went out on dates as for any fashion sense; yet the happy result was that everyone called her "Jackie" in the belief that she was a devotee trying to mimic the First Lady's impeccable stylishness.

   Not long after "Jackie's" hair fiasco, I had one of my own. It also concerned a wig of sorts -a waist-length ponytail, in fact -which I bought to wear while dancing and singing my way around the University of Michigan Varsity swimming pool in a drama-department production of Aristophanes' *The Frogs*.For frolicking in a toga, the add-on, or fall, was fine. What was *not* fine was that I saved it and on those "bad hair days" after college would occasionally wind it around my own short ponytail, hoping for a look that was very Audrey Hepburn in *Breakfast at Tiffany's*when in fact, what I'd actually achieved was neo-Madame Nu. Nor did I calculate far enough in advance in deciding when to wear this fall. And so, inevitably, I found myself in the midst of a passionate assignation, getting up from bed while my hairpiece remained behind. It had gone the way of so many of those 60s-era false eyelashes, wayward butterflies adrift on conjugal pillows, however, this little bun simply detached itself and lay beside my sleeping paramour like an abandoned horse's tail. Returning from my ablutions, I swiftly reattached it, but never wore it again.

   Nor did either of us speak of it until many years later. By then, we had broken up, gone our separate ways, and then renewed our relationship.

One evening, laughing shyly, he brought up my hairpiece, which he remembered with considerably less delicacy than he might have, as "lying there like a big old horse's tail." Worse, he wasn't the only one. A mutual friend, whom he'd apparently regaled with the incident, *also* brought it up. "Yes, he still talks about that wig," she laughed, repeating him word for word, "Lying in his bed like a big old horse's tail." Ha ha.

Let's be frank. What would you do when confronted with such a recollection? Probably you'd be mature and well-adjusted, and you'd laugh louder and longer than either friend (or at the very least, you'd give an amicable little trill). Well, I wasn't, and I didn't. Instead, I did the only thing I could. I lied. "You're thinking of someone else," I assured my former Romeo. "He's getting me mixed up with another woman." I insisted to my friend.

That hairpiece had transformed itself into a hair shirt, a penance for my vanity. Yet which was worse? Confusing me with another woman in the sack? Or *not* confusing me, and thinking that my perfectly fine tresses were so lame, so pathetic, so - (*scroungy, dirty, thick, badly cut, overdone*, you fill in the blank), that I needed to wear a really bad wig to bed?

As far as I was concerned, there was no contest.

Marjorie Rosen in the author of the books *Popcorn Venus: Women, Movies & the American Dream; Mia and Woody: Love & Betrayal*; and the novel *What Nigel Knew*. Currently, she is deputy editor at the *New York Times Magazine*'s special issues, *Women's Fashions of the Times* and *Style & Entertaining*.

HAIR TODAY...
Emily Colas

When I moved into my new place, I spent a lot of time in the apartment waiting. For the landlord to bring me the mail box key, for the cable to be hooked up, for the painters to arrive. At first it was okay. I needed to be there to clean up, unpack, settle in. But when it was the phone company's turn to visit, the woman who schedules appointments told me I needed to be at home from 8:00 a.m until 5:00 p.m.

"Can you be a little more specific?" I ask.

"Sorry. It's the best I can do."

I had already done everything I needed to in the apartment, but this being New York, I suppose there's always a fresh layer of dirt to remove. So while I waited, I swept and mopped the floors and then moved on to the tub. By ten thirty my interest in hygiene was starting to fade. I tried redecorating. I moved a couple of chairs around, put m:y bed on an angle, then put it back where it was. Next I had a snack, an apple and some peanut butter and thought about all the people I wanted to call but couldn't. Now it was eleven. I read some of my book, flipped through the TV channels and then got up to look for the Bell Atlantic van out the window. I saw all the free people down there, walking the streets and it was then that I noticed it was quite possibly the most beautiful day ever. I was so frustrated I did the only thing then that I knew to do. I went to the bathroom, took out the scissors and cut myself bangs. It wasn't as impulsive as it sounds. I'd been thinking about doing it for a while. Even mentioned it a few times to my hairdresser. But our conversations always went something like this:

I'd say, "I think I want to try bangs."

He'd get this horrified book on his face and say, "No! That would be a huge mistake."

And then I'd leave defeated. 'Well, I showed him," I thought. Looking in the mirror, getting all cocky. "He can't tell me what to do with my hair. He doesn't own me." While those thoughts looped in my head I kept cutting and wiping up the strands that feel to the floor, then cutting more. I got madder and madder. So I cut and I cleaned and I cut and I cleaned and ...

"OH MY GOD!"

The only way to rationalize this new look, the only thing I could figure was the combination of the waiting and the being trapped and the fumes from the cleaning products all affected my better judgment. Except now I had this sort of curtain of short bangs just sitting on my forehead. I had to admit that I needed my hairdresser, but how could I face him? He'd be so hurt. Another's scissors had touched my head. It would be like taking your child to see a Van Gough and he draws on it with crayons and then try-ing to explain what happened. "It's like this Vincent, sure your picture was pretty and all, it's just, well, we thought it needed a little finessing."

I tried to think up a good story. Like I had leaned over a lit candle and the front section of my hair caught on fire and it happened to burn off in a row of bangs. Or it got so damaged from all the blowing and straightening I do that it just broke off. But how could I lie? Hadn't I done enough damage.

I didn't call, but instead just showed up at his salon. Hoping the shock of seeing me would elicit pity rather than smack of betrayal. But he's a pro. I didn't need to worry. He sat me down in his chair, draped the protective smock over me and said reassuringly, 'They're just a little heavy. I'll tighten them up." I closed my eyes and he snipped furiously and when he was done, he studied my face in the mirror and proclaimed, "It works now." Then he even got in the spirit of the new look, "Maybe we could dye the bangs a different color. What do you think?"

So now I find myself waiting again. This time for my bangs to grow back. I've got a long road ahead of me, but the way I figure it, they serve as a reminder. To both be a more patient person, and perhaps more importantly, to never ever again be disloyal to my hairdresser.

Emily Colas is the author of *Just Checking: Scenes From the Life of an Obsessive Compulsive*. In her spare time, she attempts to complete all the *New York Magazine* crossword puzzles ever published, religiously watches the Oprah Winfrey Show, and pretends to be working on her second book.

HAIR AND HEALTH
Richard Stein

Recently I was cutting the hair of an old friend; this is a special relationship which spans over the many years that I've been styling and changing her looks through many of her most important acting assignments. She's a well-known, high profile performer and our sessions together are always intense because of the importance of getting the look just right. We were interrupted in the middle of the haircut by the receptionist of the salon who came over and announced to me that I had a very important. phone call, when I inquired as to whom it was she told me that it was another client requesting information about a wig for a relative who was soon to have chemotherapy. I told her that I would return the call as soon as I could and went back to the task at hand. My friend began asking me questions about wigs and chemotherapy and what and how one had to do to go about the process. I distractedly answered her as I continued to work on my creation little knowing until the following Sunday, when she called me at home, to tell me that she herself had been diagnosed with a serious form of cancer and would I help her find a wig.

Over the years I've become increasingly dismayed by how little information is known about cancer, chemotherapy, and women's hair. I've tried to develop a kind of we-can-get-through-this attitude with the women I've encountered at the early stages of their illness because I truly believe that there is a strong connection between self-confidence in the way one looks and the healing process.

Suggesting gently to someone to cut off their locks as soon as possible to prepare them for what eventually may happen isn't easy particularly if that woman is attached to her hair. All sorts of unasked-for changes will occur. There's suddenly going to be a major style shift, one's natural hair color revealed, just to name a few. Each woman's wig needs are different;

my actress mend ended up with two wigs, each differently styled and colored, one for day and one for evening.

I remember being called at the last minute to cut the wig of a young woman I knew who was in the hospital and already undergoing strong treatments. When I arrived I found someone who literally hadn't combed her formerly thick hair in days. As I began to comb her hair it started to come out till there was virtually none left, I quickly cut the wig that her mother had purchased into the style that she was accustomed to and tried to restore her to some sort of normalcy. After I had gone, one of the nurses came into the room and admired the young woman's hair thinking it was her own. This made up for an extremely tense and difficult situation.

Things usually move very quickly after the first discovery of this particular illness, shock, grief, and rage plus numerous other emotions appears, there seems little time to focus on much, let alone getting situated properly with a new wig. However it really is an extremely important step in the healing process. Changing ones hairstyle almost always provides a lift and so it can be with a wig.

I recently had a heart-to-heart conversation with a client, a young, single, well-to-do businesswoman whose mother had just found out she had ovarian cancer; she lives in Illinois in an area not especially known for wigs. I offered to help and had her send me the best picture of herself with whatever information was pertinent, her color formula, style ideas, head size, etc. I found a relatively inexpensive wig, which I cut on the head of an employee that had a similar look to the woman. I managed to complete everything and send it off just before the first chemo treatment. The result was one ecstatic lady. She managed to wear her wig to a big family event where everyone oohed and aahed about how good she looked, even people who didn't know she was sick. She subsequently was heard to boast to people about her New York wig.

Another woman I know, during her recovery from an illness that damaged her hair, stopped wearing a wig and was sporting a growing out haircut that looked like a beautiful white halo, was stopped on the streets of Manhattan by a Japanese photographer who insisted on taking her picture raving about her hairdo as the last word in fashion. This incident buoyed the woman's confidence to no end and the comments and compliments from her friends and colleagues about her hairstyle have in large part given her the courage to continue to wear her hair in a short style long after her recovery.

I've spent most of my career encouraging my clients, men and women, to be aware of the hair health factor. Few people really understand the texture of their hair let alone what their hair needs for ongoing health. Engaging in a dialogue with one's hairdresser about the health of one's hair is just as important as finding the right style. Healthy scalp and hair is everyone's dream and most importantly everyone's right.

To Climb, Ascend, Descend, Transcend
Janet Sternburg

Joan and I greet each other with huge smiles, so very pleased to see one another after six months. I begin with something that had just come to me on the # 104 bus: "Together we've lost about three and a half pounds since we first met." For a moment, Joan doesn't get it, and responds as to a report on successful dieting. "No," I say, patting my flat left chest and looking significantly at hers, just as flat and far more recent.

Today she is looking beautiful. I'd been a bit nervous about seeing if her recently shaved head (a gesture of one-upping the inevitable) would make her look mannish. On one of our coast-to-coast phone calls, she had told me about her first venture out like this, to her local Soho cafe where she's a regular. The young crew-cutted waitress who floats around in a peignoir and Doc Martens had never paid any attention to her until she showed up bald. Suddenly the waitress began treating her as though she were cool, an interesting person after all.

It's so different from when I got sick six years ago. Body mutilation has become fashionable. A photographer at a recent symposium showed images of skin-carvings, including one of herself holding a knife to her female lover's breast. The room was packed with an admiring gathering of black leather, bright yellow hair, nose rings. I stood in the back wanting to scream, "You idiots!" A knife at a woman's breast isn't a flirtation with danger. It's an attempt to stave off death.

Joan and I order coffee. I haul a shopping bag onto the cafe table and begin lying out a stack of scarves, flipping through them like pages of a well-thumbed book. The top one I'd recently laundered, a soft blush pink of Egyptian cotton with an ivory border. I'd ironed it especially to show

how much more attractive the rest of the scarves will eventually look, even though most of them have been in my drawer for years.

I call them The Kate Wasserman Headcovering Collection, a fond remembrance of how, when I first learned that I had to have chemotherapy, my friends sprung into action, delivering Kate to my door. Lovely Kate who had laid her head one night on her pillow and awakened to a bed in flames, later to a badly burned head which required a series of skin grafts. A woman of style and panache, Kate had invested in a remarkable panoply of head coverings.

To Joan I now show a black and white and yellow silk scarf with the initials YSL; a purple cotton triangle rimmed with gilt coins, exotic once on Kate's wide-boned face but too much for my own gypsy-ish features. From India, a hand-blocked print, burnt orange entwined with magenta, and a wrinkly turquoise scarf dotted with tiny mirrors. Next, a navy and white striped cotton square, quite smart, quite French, Jean Seberg crossed with Catherine Deneuve. A long scarf, rust-colored, with a Native American arrow motif.

I should have returned these scarves to Kate, now thriving in marriage, motherhood, and good work. But instead, I'm passing them on to Joan who, beautiful though she looks, is quite ill, at least if one judges by the number of affected lymph nodes. Hers were double mine. She's receiving chemotherapy through a drip catheter installed under her collarbone, less vein-scarring than when I received it through my hand once a month. Pulling down the collar of her blouse, Joan shows me the incision. I wince: it looks like it hurts, and it does.

Joan and I reach a point in our conversation when the thing to do is disappear into the ladies room and show each other our scars, which are more or less the same, allowing for her still-inflamed redness and the slightly more hollow dent of mine. I show her my ravishing new bra of which I am so proud, with its black lace that lets both the real and the prosthetic breast peep through. With the prosthesis slipped into its pocket like a visiting card into a glove, no one would guess I'm faking it.

It's time to leave, I'm going uptown to a show at the Guggenheim Museum. We stand outside the plate-glass window of the cafe, and I find myself reaching over to pat Joan's cheek, a gesture that reminds me of something my grandmother might have done. Then I'm seized with love.

In the great spiral hall of the museum, I stand for a long time looking at a piece of the contemporary German artist, Rebecca Horn. She has strung a wire from ceiling to floor. Along its length, a beat-up brown suitcase travels, ascending and descending while it slowly opens and shuts. Prayer, so often evoked in her work through that gesture of slowly coming together, again and again, like palms needing to touch.

Janet Sternburg is the author of the memoir *Phantom Limb*. She is also the author and editor of both volumes of *The Writer on Her Work*. A widely published poet and essayist, she is acknowledged as a pioneer in creating new ways to present literature on stage and film. A visual artist as well, her photography is in private and museum collections.

HAIR AND GRACE
Richard Stein

Originally this piece was to be called "Hair and Aging," but to me the word "aging" has acquired unfortunate cultural connotations. Even in this hopeful new millennium, most fashion and beauty magazines, and their all-important advertisers, have continued stubbornly to write off anyone over thirty-five, preferring to maintain the myth of the Youth Culture.

With age should come wisdom, serenity, and grace. Yet even extensive experience with ones hair over the years does not necessarily afford laser insight into its possibilities. On the contrary, a cherished hairstyle can actually blind a woman to new hair horizons, effectively imprisoning her in a kind of style time warp -trendy at thirty, dated at forty.

And as for the fifties, nothing so preoccupies most women poised on the cusp of the half-century than that plaguey question: to gray or not to gray. The belief that gray hair ages a woman is deeply embedded in the collective unconscious. We are bombarded by those beguiling TV ads, with beautiful, perennially-young models, telling us that getting rid of the gray is just a shampoo away. The subliminal message is seductive. Simply coloring our hair will subtract any number of years from our calendar and stymie the dread aging process, keeping time at bay.

The whole issue of color is a complicated one, but my own position is clear. For the most part I do not encourage people to do it unless it's a career necessity (for actors, for politicians, for spokespeople). Coloring has a profound impact, both physical and psychological. Physically, it's "once colored, long-time colored." It can seem to take forever for an unfortunate new hue to grow out. Psychologically, it's obsession time. Was or wasn't it the right decision in the first place?

I'm convinced that the silhouette -the way the hair is shaped to the dimension of the head - is the crucial element in a successful hairstyle. Still, even I'll admit that coloring can be an added adornment to beautifully-cut hair, but it's important for both stylist and client to bear in mind that the true art of color lies in subtlety. Often ones color looks best on the eve of redoing. It's then that I encourage a woman to be patient. Just wait a little longer. Let a new hair cut complement the old color to produce a fresh effect. That stubborn hobgoblin, consistency, dictates sticking with a tried and true look, but when a woman learns more about her particular style range, as she matures -dare I say "ages?" I do! -she may also gain the confidence to experiment -even if that means not using any color at all.

The beauty and grace of the aging process is the ability to see ourselves in a new way -as a work-in-creative-progress -and not to be hurried into changing for the sake of change. As a woman's relationship with her hair evolves over time, hopefully, so does her comfort level. With self-knowledge and self-confidence comes courage. The challenge to sympathetic stylist and courageous client, working and communicating in harmony, becomes creating a distinctive hairstyle, a highly personal and flexible look, one tethered to a woman's accurate sense of herself – of her uniqueness – and not to the look of the day.

The Hairs
Sharon Olds

At 53, I start to save the hairs from my comb, and from the rug by the bureau, a and to keep them in a bowl, and then, at night, when the wind is from the east, to loose them out the western window, over the park, for the nests -longing for some part of me, a stream of keratin from near my brain, to be used by one who cannot fall to hell, who files and lays, and along the oval portmanteau of the offspring lays species-telltale splotches, squighiggles, dawdles, dodder, doodles, duty-off waste-free songings of the female body.

At 53, 1/2, I stop, not only because a man at a party when I ask if anyone else does this, says, So that's where all that gunk is coming from, axle-winding the gears and cogs of the working world -but because I fear that my beloved might find one of these nests of nest-questing silver and feel, perhaps, his first disgust at the mortal, at me. But at 53 11/12, when I see a troop of flitting dashing cometing meteoring cupids in a low tree, I take my little mess to them. This is what I have made, tiny mothers, with my body, my scalp, these quirked rivulets like handleable, passable-down, polished tears, of joy, or of grief, or something exertion of bliss or necessary work just the streaks of energy, as I use up my life.

Sharon Olds is a Poet Laureate of New York State. Her works include *Satan Says, The Dead and the Living, The Gold Cell, The Father, The Wellspring* and *Blood, Tin, Straw*.

The Problem of the Mirror
Louise Gluck

The problem of the salon is the problem of the mirror. This isn't to say that reflecting surfaces are, in general, a difficulty in the world, or that the self lives in terror of what confirms the pathos of its physical shell: the panoramic windows of large cities, the backs of spoons, and so on. Narcissism, being essentially self-protective, learns early to negotiate reflection, or at least to do so under most conditions.

By the age of six or seven I had mastered my angles. I knew how to stand to best advantage, how far from the glass, in what position relative to light. I could manipulate, in the mirror, the antecedents of soft focus: dusk, early evening. These were tropisms, daily actions: they occurred without thought. They were also solitary: their aim was a truce with the body; that such a truce relied on manipulation or guile seemed entirely acceptable. And only when another form of looking at the self, a form that diminished control, presented itself did these rituals begin to seem a subject for meditation.

The narcissist who, daily, makes his or her peace with the mirror engages in a kind of dialogue; the absence of witnesses stands for the absence of a real world. If, in these private encounters, all evasions and canny poses and aesthetic adjustments fail to produce an acceptable reflection, one can look away, ending the encounter, erasing the unsatisfying body. Whereas the gaze of a witness affirms these moments as what they really are: defeat of imagination by the physical self.

No form of this interaction seems to me more brutal than what occurs in the salon, its luxury, its intention to minister notwithstanding. The chair at its fixed height, the terrible light of Madison Avenue streaming in at the worst possible angle, augmented by the savage lights above the mirror.

And all around the sort of beauty designed to survive this environment. Movement, adjustment, isn't permitted: if the head isn't stable and fixed, if illumination isn't permitted: if the head isn't stable and fixed, if illumination isn't sharp, the hair can't be accurately cut. And as the head is fixed, the eyes are forced into protracted confrontation, the gaze met by not one but two gazes. At every moment, the replica of the self, so mercilessly undefended, is being regarded by someone outside the self (the self so ready with its arsenal of denials), regarded by the cool professional. His training, of course, means he will say nothing, make no comment on what we both watch. No comment, only a few soothing murmurs. Not too many: too many would seem insistent. Because this particular professional is clever (of mind as well as with scissors) he chooses exchange of another kind. He diverts, distracts. Or he is quiet, recognizing how hopeless any attempt to transform ordeal to pleasure must be.

Very little of this is the humiliation of growing older. In my adolescence, in my twenties, I kept my hair long, as long as thin brittle hair would grow. Partly I hated change; principally I felt unequal to the salon. To watch the self in the presence of another, who also watched, to feel fantasy and delusion exposed by that second gaze: even at my least blemished, this seemed to me to dramatize the pitiful discrepancy between what I wished to be and what I was.

Decades later, I go through these sessions because I recognize, afterward, the benefits accrued. In any case, vanity seems a mechanism to be closely examined, in preparation for the assaults of time.

But how amazingly unvaried the whole process. First, the building anxiety. Then the guile, the strategies (wearing no makeup so the pathos of appearance can be ascribed to a cause). The early arrival (hope of dismissal, attempt to translate mutual confusion about the time of the appointment into actual deferral). And then the misery of the actual event.

And afterward, such an eager courting of reflection, such a rich renewed infatuation with the little silver self, a love not in the least dependent on corroboration or endorsement. Because none of this is about the world. It concerns the self, in all its disdainful pride. The self, with its ancient craving to be manifest in a body it can esteem and embrace.

Louise Gluck is the Pulitzer Prize winning author of *Wild Iris* and other fine works including *Firstborn, The House on Marshland, Descending Figure, The Triumph of Achilles, Ararat, Proofs and Theories: Essays on Poetry* and *Meadowlands*. She is the current Poet Laureate of the United States.

When I Went Gray Over My Summer Vacation
Dr. Ruth K. Westheimer

Though I don't put any store in astrology, the fact is that I'm a Gemini so that it probably wouldn't surprise some people that I might have two sides to particular issues.

Part of me is what I like to call a "kibbutznik," which resulted from having worked on a kibbutz when I was living in Israel as a young woman. That side of me abhors wearing make-up or wasting time styling my hair or picking out the right outfit. The "kibbutznik" in me feels that looks take second place to what feels comfortable.

The other side of me is what I call my "Pierre-ish" look. When I first became Dr. Ruth, my minister of communications, Pierre Lehu, used to ask me what I was wearing or whether I'd gone to the beauty parlor before giving an interview. At first I thought he was crazy for asking such questions, bit I soon got used to the fancy clothes and having people fussing about my head, styling my hair and covering my face with what I still refer to as "that gunk." I had come to the conclusion that if my face was going to be seen by millions of people, even I, the "kibbutznik" retained enough vanity to want to look my best.

Having been turned blond by my hair stylists in the past, even though I hated the coloring process, I continued to put myself through it because I had an image to maintain. But during the summer of 1997 I came to a different conclusion.

My husband had passed away in April. I had two grandchildren with a third on the way. I had a new book about grandparents coming out in the Fall. I spent the summer in Israel, the land of the kibbutz, as well as Russia and Uzbekistan, working on a documentary about grandparents. I was full of energy and very busy and just didn't want to have to worry about going to the hair dresser. I made the decision to go gray.

I loved being gray. This was the real me. Just as being blond hadn't really made me any younger, being gray didn't make me any older. I retained the same old zip and if I still left people half my age dragging along after me, why did I need to dye my hair?

Now I knew that when I returned I would take some flak. First of all, there were my children. And then, there was Pierre. But even if they complained, and they did, I knew I could handle them. The one person who causes me the most concern, however, was my hair stylist, Richard Stein.

Since I don't pay that much attention to the way I look, I rely very heavily on the experts whom I allow to take charge of these matters. If Richard had said to me, "Ruth, you can't be seen on the streets of New York looking like this," I probably would have given in. I would have been a little sad, but I'd been blond for the last dozen years, so it wouldn't have been a total stranger looking back at me in the mirror.

But rather than disparage my new look, Richard was very supportive. Of course he couldn't wait to get his hands on my head in order to cut and style those silver and gray strands of mine, which he ordered me to call "platinum," but he immediately sensed how happy my natural look made me and didn't even try to convince me to color my hair.

Now I don't really know if Richard's attitude was based more on his skills as a psychologist than on his aesthetic views, but I have no intention of delving into his psyche to try to find out. I'm just thrilled that I can walk into his salon as often as I want to have my hair styled without fear of reproach.

Dr. Ruth Westheimer has written 18 books. They include *Dr. Ruth's Encyclopedia of Sex, Dr. Ruth's Pregnancy Guide for Couples, The Art of Arousal, Dr. Ruth Talks to Kids* and *Rekindling Romance for Dummies*.

www.ingramcontent.com/pod-product-compliance
Lightning Source LLC
Chambersburg PA
CBHW042129010526
44111CB00031B/33